Changed in a Moment

by
Randy Clark

Changed in a Moment:
The Far-reaching Effects of Impartation Prayer

© Copyright 2010, Global Awakening
All rights reserved

Compiled by: Phillip Olson

Edited by: Susan Fleming and Lisa Lindle

No part of this book may be reproduced, stored, or transmitted in any form or by any means, electronic or mechanical, including photocopying and recording, or by any information storage or retrieval system, except as may be expressly permitted in writing by the publisher. Requests for permission should be addressed in writing to:

Global Awakening
1451 Clark St
Mechanicsburg, PA 17055

Unless otherwise noted, Scripture quotations are taken from HOLY BIBLE, NEW INTERNATIONAL VERSION®. Copyright © 1973, 1978, 1984 by International Bible Society. Used by permission of Zondervan Publishing House.

Scripture quotations marked (NASB) are taken from the NEW AMERICAN STANDARD BIBLE®, Copyright © 1960, 1962, 1963, 1971, 1972, 1973, 1975, 1977, 1995 by The Lockman Foundation. Used by permission.

Scripture quotations marked (NKJV) are taken from the New King James Version®. Copyright © 1982 by Thomas Nelson, Inc. Used by permission. All rights reserved. NKJV is a trademark of Thomas Nelson, Inc.

Table of Contents

Introduction 1

Carol Baerg - Missionary at Large 5

Bob Bradberry and Will Hart - Fishers of Men 13

Drenda Lalor - Freed and Restored 17

Carter Wood - Anointed, Activated, and Commissioned 29

Mark Anderson - Empowered for Evangelism in India 51

Robert Devens - Turbocharged for Miracles 59

Don Foster - Ministering in Power in Mozambique 83

George - Brain Tumor Victim Turned Victor 93

Pete and Jenna - Called Out and Raised Up for Asia 129

Endnote 165

Introduction

Changed in a Moment is long overdue. Published nearly a decade and a half ago, my first book, *God Can Use Little Ole Me,* was a gathering of stories from early in the outpouring of the Spirit in the mid-1990's. It was simply a compilation of the remarkable stories of ordinary people. Their testimonies were amazing and uplifting. They still are.

This book is not technical, theological, or complicated, but do not underestimate its power to affect your life. As you read it, I pray you will experience your own "change in a moment." I pray that you will receive an understanding of grace, a gift of faith, and a baptism of love. I pray that you will change your thinking about God. I pray you will come to see Him as the loving Father who is good and whose mercy endures forever. I pray you will know Him as He is, not as the one behind tragedy, the so-called "acts of God," which aren't really acts of God, but the result of the work of His enemies and our own self-inflected, destructive choices. May His goodness lead you to change what you believe about Him. May you be touched by His power and His goodness.

Changed in a Moment shares new stories that demonstrate to believers that God is still doing today what He was doing more than 15 years ago. I remain amazed at the power of God to radically change a person's life in a matter of seconds. There are people who are desperate from terminal illness or a lifetime of sickness, but suddenly, by just one touch of His Spirit, they are healed and then called to their own healing ministry.

Or there is the successful young vice president of a bank who had achieved the American dream—a large, fine home, very expensive cars, a successful career with a great salary, and a beautiful wife. Yet with just one touch of God's power, he found his life turned upside down. So did his wife, who fell to the floor beside him- they went down as nominal Christians and rose as changed, on fire, deeply committed Christians. This man's priorities, values and goals were totally changed in a matter of a few minutes while he lay on the floor, resting in the power of God. This couple's story is mind-boggling.

I am thrilled to get these exciting, encouraging testimonies into your hands. Our human minds find it difficult to explain the changes in these people's lives. When I began my studies at Oakland City University almost 40 years ago, I remember one of my Religious Studies professors saying, "It isn't as important how high you jump, as it is how you walk when you land." He was referring to the custom in some country Baptist churches of people jumping or shouting when touched by the Holy Spirit. Today we might rephrase this statement as, "It isn't as important how long you lay on the floor, or how hard you laughed in the Spirit, or how greatly you trembled, as it is how you walk afterwards." Your life should reflect your commitment, dedication, and consecration to Christ.

This book does not emphasize phenomena so much as it does changed lives. It's not about shaking but changing, not about falling to the floor but falling in love with God anew, not about having your eyes opened to see the angelic or demonic but having your eyes opened to see the needs of family and neighbors, and not so much about going to heaven as going to the nations. In writing this book, I wanted to help us understand what happens to someone who experiences such a radical change in his or her life. What do they feel physically, what communication do they receive from God that would so redirect their lives? Or we might ask, where does this new love for others come from? Perhaps it is time for a new *Varieties of Religious Experience* to be written. I am not sure William James truly understood the experiences he examined in his famous book.

Join me as we seek to understand the profoundness of being "changed in a moment" by God. I hope you will be moved to tears of love and joyous laughter, and at the same time experience a profound peace as you read about those who have been touched by the Prince of Peace. Read about their battles of faith and how just one touch set in motion a new life definitely touched by God. We have purposely chosen stories of men and women, of professionals and blue-collar workers, of pastors, missionaries and laypeople.

My friend, Pastor Bill Johnson, has a famous teaching on the "Power of the Testimony" which communicates the truth of Revelation 19:10, "For the testimony of Jesus is the spirit of prophecy."[1] He shares that a testimony of what Jesus has done for someone carries with it a prophetic invitation for that sign, wonder, or miracle to be repeated in the listener's life. May many be healed and touched by His presence as they read these prophetic invitations for God to do again what He has done before. Please let us know about your "change" by heaven's touch. Write us at goglobal@globalawakening.com. We would love to read emails telling about your touch.

In the 17 years since the Holy Spirit fell in Toronto, people who were dramatically touched have come to tell me their stories—of new life in the Spirit, of new physical life. January 20, 1994, was the beginning of the outpouring of the Holy Spirit in Toronto, Ontario,

---

[1] NIV

Canada. These meetings became the longest protracted meetings in the history of Western Civilization. They continued for more than 12 years, six nights per week.

On that first night, I remember praying for a woman named Carole. God touched her, and she was resting in her seat, experiencing His presence. I heard the impression from the Holy Spirit, "Go back and tell her she has been sad too long." When I stood in front of her, I felt impressed to form my hand as if it were a pitcher and told her to drink, saying, "God says you have been sad too long." She was immediately overwhelmed with joy and drunkenness that continued for a long time. She continued to have these experiences frequently for years after. I was shocked when I found out why she had been so sad for so long, and why she now had such joy. I am encouraged to share with you that which God did for Carole he has done for thousands more, rescuing them from sickness and disease, and using them to bring the healing love of God to others. Let's begin with Carole Baerg and her story.

Carole Baerg
Missionary at Large

It was January 1994. I had just heard the news!

A Vineyard pastor named Randy Clark had been invited by John Arnott to come to share at the church he pastored in Toronto. John Arnott had heard Randy speak at a Vineyard leaders' meeting about how he had received a powerful impartation through the ministry of Rodney Howard-Browne. I had watched a few television broadcasts covering Rodney Howard-Browne's meetings. Those meetings were becoming known as "The Laugh Revival." Was the "Laugh Revival" coming to Toronto?

I had nothing to laugh about. In fact, I had every reason to feel sad- very sad!

After graduating from nursing school in St. Catharine's, Ontario, Canada, I enrolled at Moody Bible Institute in Chicago to become a missionary nurse. After completing one year at Moody, I experienced many challenges to my faith, and I left Christianity to pursue a nursing career in Chicago. I did very well and became the head nurse of the Orthopaedic wing at the University of Chicago Hospital.

However, a bad accident a few years later left me with serious injuries. While awaiting a surgical procedure that could leave me paralyzed, I was challenged to pray and ask God to show Himself to me by healing me. I prayed in the middle of the next night, God healed me, and I left the hospital without surgery. I then came back to God. As part of my reconciliation with my earthly father, I asked him what he wanted me to do. My father asked me to return home to St. Catharine's. I obeyed my father and returned home.

Shortly after my return to Canada, I began to experience an increasing number of cases of flu, colds, and lung infections. In 1974, I was diagnosed with an immune disease and given three to four months to live. By miracle and grace and much prayer, I lived mostly bedridden until the fall of 1993. At that point, I was tired of the pain and the exhaustion of constantly struggling against the disease, and I was ready to be with Jesus. My body was failing. It became more and more difficult for my body to produce enough antibodies. Even a small cut on a finger took a long time to heal. I was hospitalized often for intravenous antibiotic treatments and oxygen therapy.

Although I had survived for twenty years, my prognosis was not good. In fact, I was tired of fighting for my life and was beginning to think that it would be better to be with Jesus. One doctor felt I had a very short time to live. I was invited to share a home with very close friends who provided me with a comfortable place to spend the last weeks of my life. Their children called me "Nanna," and they were very special to me.

But, God had other plans!

As we drove off to the first meetings where Randy Clark was going to share, I was filled with strange expectations. There were perhaps 120 people present, and it seemed to me that it was like any other Charismatic meeting that I had attended. At the end of the service, people were getting prayer. I was not that impressed with what I saw. With disappointment, I approached my friends who had brought me with them. They asked me if I had received prayer. My response was, "Prayer for what?" I was quickly advised to find Randy and ask him to pray for me. Reluctantly, I approached him.

Randy really did not pray for me like I expected or had experienced in the past. He took my hands, looked at me, and said, "There is enough sadness in the church, and you have been sad long enough." I found myself down on the floor on my hands and knees laughing.

My body might have been on the floor, but I was "caught up" in an amazing vision. I found myself in heaven where God the Father was hosting a party. There were banquet tables loaded with an abundance of every delicacy possible. In addition, there were barrels and barrels of wine. Everyone was happy, laughing, and enjoying themselves. Jesus Himself was pouring this New Wine. He encouraged me to drink, "More." I felt my mouth being opened and wine being poured in. We were indeed having a wonderful time.

After a while, all I could see in this vision was a huge wine glass. There were three very distinct characteristics of this massive container. First, everyone could drink at the same time. Second, as you drank, you also could get a shower. And third, everyone present could climb into this goblet and play in this New Wine.

No one had ever informed me that we could have fun and laugh in the presence of the Holy Spirit. I was taught that God was very serious, and that the Spirit-filled life was very serious. The Christian life was hard, disciplined, but necessary to get to heaven. What a surprise! All through this time, I laughed and laughed while I kicked and banged the floor.

This vision ended when Jesus carried me and placed me on the knee of my Heavenly Father. I felt His heart beat as I fell asleep.

When it was time to go home, my friends tried to wake me up. I had actually fallen asleep on the floor of the church. Never in my life had I been drunk on wine, liquor, or any other substance. I could never lose that much control. I had never seen anyone "drunk in the Spirit." I tried to get up, but I could not stand. All I could do was laugh. I was the first to be carried out of those meetings, so overcome by the Spirit that I could not walk. I was totally inebriated on the love of Jesus. I felt wonderful!

When I awakened the next morning, I felt the same as I had when I crawled into bed the night before. What really surprised me was the realization that I had fallen asleep and slept all night. I suffered from chronic insomnia. The experience the night before remained very real. I felt as safe and affirmed as I had when I rested on my Father's knee. I was overwhelmed by a deep and very powerful love. This was not just a 'passing experience,' but a deep encounter with the Holy Spirit that gave me a deep hunger and an overwhelming passion for more. This was, for sure, the abundant life. I spent the next few months in this wonderful condition.

Suddenly, life became exciting! We could hardly wait to get to the next meeting to see what would happen. It was all far beyond my wildest imagination!

After a few days, I noticed that I had not taken my usual medication. The horrible headaches were gone. I was sleeping at night, and I felt totally energized. I was not only excited about life and living, but very excited about what the Holy Spirit was doing.

Every evening I lined up for another touch and would then rest on the floor for long periods of time. The presence of Jesus was so strong that it was always hard to get up. My hands would become very red and burning hot. My feet would feel like they were on fire. Randy instructed us not to be too quick to get up, but to ask the Holy

Spirit to minister and speak to us. And He did!

Two weeks after the "Laugh Revival" began, I attended a women's conference with my close friend in another city. Friends who knew of my illness were surprised to see me there. During the first meeting, I was asked to come up and share what had happened to me. As I tried to speak and even stand up to share, I felt it all happening again. I lost total control, became very drunk in the Spirit, and could not stop laughing. It was then that we discovered that this was transferable. One could "pass it on." Ladies asked me to "bless them" with what I had received and they also experienced this incredible joy. What fun!

We attended as many meetings as possible. No one wanted the meetings to stop. John Arnott extended the meetings, and Randy Clark stayed. Soon, people were coming in from around the world to see what was happening. We wanted to receive as much as we could get.

The voice of the Holy Spirit became so clear to me. One evening after crawling off the floor, I sat on a chair near the front of the room. Randy came by and blessed me with "More, Lord." My mouth was already wide open, and I could not shut it. I heard a voice clearly say, "You open your mouth, and I will fill it."

Another time after I was blessed with "more," I saw horses lined up in front of a huge gate in a vast courtyard. These horses pounded the stones with their hooves, anxious to run. The gates suddenly swung open, and the horses stampeded out with grim determination in their eyes. What a surprise when I realized that I was on the front horse. It was a large white stallion without saddle, bit, or bridle. I was leaning into his strong neck and holding onto his mane. We were off! I did not know where we were off to, but we were riding with great speed and strength. The stallion carried me. I did not command him.

As more and more people gathered each night, I continued to experience the Presence and the Power of the Holy Spirit. My hunger for more only increased. In another one of those early meetings, I saw myself on a rubber raft or dinghy in the middle of a river. I was very puzzled because I do not swim, and I do not like water. I tried to paddle to the shore with my hands, but I was trapped in a whirlpool going round and round. This river was dangerous. Panic took over as I realized that this river was the mighty Niagara River! Suddenly, the raft catapulted out of the whirlpool, and the strong currents carried me down the river. Where was this river taking me?

Almost from the beginning, I was asked to be part of the ministry team at the revival meetings. I blessed people as I had been blessed, and people received. When I touched them, others too were overwhelmed by the Spirit.

Within weeks I was asked to travel with my close friends to various places and share my story. More and more doors opened up. I saw people healed and encouraged, and the Holy Spirit empowered their lives. In the summer of 1994, we travelled to Minnesota for the first time; by December, we were invited to Holland and Belgium.

Since that time I have been symptom-free and have travelled constantly, ministering. Although I never married, I have many spiritual children who call me "Nanna" because of my love for them and because of what God has done in them.

I personally discovered that impartation blesses what God wants to do. It enables people to hear for themselves and calls forth individual destiny. All of us have been born to make a difference. The powerful impartation I received in Toronto has overcome sickness, disease, and other hindrances in my life.

God set me free from strong religious barriers, and I could hear, see, and feel Him for myself. Negative words spoken over me disappeared. In the past I had been told that I was only a woman, and single too, so that I really could not do much. The Holy Spirit set me free to be a mighty woman of God. I was brought to life, and life became abundant and more exciting than I could have imagined.

The strong current of that mighty river has taken me to many places since those beginning days of renewal in January 1994. It has become a very exciting ride, and prophetic words and dreams have become a reality.

I love to encourage people everywhere I go. If He could do it for me, He can do it for anyone. My Heavenly Father has a very big knee, and He has a place for everyone. My desire is to see individuals everywhere set on fire with a burning passion for Jesus. I want to see young and old alike free to fulfill their destiny.

It is hard for me to even acknowledge the scope and power of my own ministry. Often when I return to places where I have ministered previously, I hear reports of what the Spirit has done after a previous visit, and it is often a very big surprise.

I minister in churches of many different denominations. Besides preaching in church settings, I also have the privilege of ministering in youth meetings, youth conferences, women's meetings and conferences. In addition, I teach in various ministry schools, university campus ministries and retreats, as well as leaders' meetings. One of my favorite places to minister is in a high security prison, and I also do a lot of visiting in various homes where I have been invited to pray for individuals in their own setting.

My ministry also includes assisting with household chores, such as caring for small children, doing the laundry, ironing clothes, and helping with meal preparation and clean-up. These "menial" tasks are also ministry. I do not stay in hotels. I travel alone and stay in private homes. As a result, I get to really know the leaders and the people, and they get to know me. This has made my ministry even more amazing. And now many of my best friends are all around the world.

A most recent joy for me has been to visit and sit with clergy in their private offices and their homes. From my religious past, I had always felt that leaders were on a very high pedestal, and lil' ole me surely had nothing to say to them. How wrong that is. What a lot of encouragement they need! It is an awesome privilege to share life, to be an encouragement and also to be encouraged.

Releasing the prophetic, moving in words of knowledge and in discernment and praying for the sick is amazing. It is wonderful to bless everyone in every meeting where I minister with the impartation that I have received. The anointing of the Holy Spirit that I received has only increased and taken me to many places in the world.

I could boast in many experiences and in many angelic visitations. But I delight to boast in the power of the Cross! Impartation has set me free to be all that He created me to be, to follow and obey Him, to know Him and the power of His resurrection working in my life. Seeing His power through signs and wonders is wonderful. The greatest miracle of all, though, is seeing people come to give their lives to Jesus. I want these days to be days of great harvest, where we see lives transformed.

I am looking forward to this next season and am filled again with great anticipation and wonder as to what is going to happen next. We owe the world an encounter with this Jesus.

What a privilege it is to have my life healed and impacted by the love of Jesus for such a time as this!

Bob Bradberry and Will Hart
Fishers of Men

Next, I want to share with you the stories of Bob Bradberry and Will Hart. Bob Bradberry was a commercial fisherman, an Episcopalian. He was a captain, had his own fishing boat, his own airplane to spot fish, and his own boat-building business. In 1994, he was making well over $200,000 a year.

He was a rough, hooked-nose New Englander from Galilee, Rhode Island, a really tough guy. He served as a catcher at several of my meetings. At one event, during the message, he began to weep. He had a strong impression from God: "Lay down your nets and come follow Me." He did.

When he was 57 years old, earning $200,000-plus a year, he sold everything. He went into his house, sat down with the Yellow Pages, and started calling every pastor in the community including nearby Providence. He just said, "Hey, my name is Bob Bradberry. I am supposed to start preaching. Can I come to your church and preach?"

The churches wanted to know about his experience. He said, "I don't have any. I am a commercial fisherman." They asked about his background. He said, "I am an Episcopalian." They asked why he wanted to come and preach. He said, "God told me to."

Can you imagine the rejection he experienced? But he did not give up. He had a tremendous anointing, especially for youth. When he spoke, even the children wept. He heard God's call, and he followed.

When Captain Bob preached, people were drawn to the same Master who called him. One of them was a young man named Will. He had grown up in an evangelical home, but had since backslidden and gotten into the Gothic culture; black fingernails, black around the eyes, black jacket, black everything. He was in New England when Captain Bob showed up to preach about the kingdom of God, the reality of God, and the power of God. The power of God shook Will, and he got saved.

Soon after, Will was on an airplane with Captain Bob, missing his high school graduation to go to Peru. Despite the fact that he had flunked Spanish in high school, he went to Peru and Captain Bob dropped him off in an area where no one spoke English. After six months, Will spoke Spanish fluently and met the woman he was going to marry. Captain Bob came to me and told me that 80 percent of the people that Will was praying for in Peru were getting healed. He asked me to take Will as one of my interns, and I did.

After three years, Will and his wife Musey led a team for us to Mozambique to work with Roland and Heidi Baker. Heidi wrote to me and said, "Randy, I need Will and Musey. They are so anointed and so good. I need them. Will you give them to me?" I said, "If they want to go." It kind of bummed me out because I was hoping I could keep him for myself.

But Will is brave, and God is using him. He went into the Congo and preached the message to a company of soldiers with their AK-47's and rocket launchers. He sent me pictures of these men weeping, their guns laid off to the side when the Spirit of God fell on them.

Drenda Lalor
Freed and Restored

In the spring of 1995, I was praying to die. For days I had lain on the carpet in the guest bedroom and cried out, "Lord, if you won't heal me, kill me. I don't want to live another day like this." I had been put on a three-month medical leave from my job as an assistant principal in a middle school and, with two weeks left to go, I was still sick. In addition to that, now I felt hopeless and abandoned by God.

For almost thirty years I had suffered from excruciating migraines. These attacks would be accompanied by violent and continuous vomiting. I would crawl to the toilet and heave until yellow bile would be the only thing left coming out of my stomach. I could not eat during these attacks, or even take in water without throwing it up; sometimes I would get dehydrated and end up in the ER. It was as if my body had been poisoned. These attacks would last three to four days, during which I was confined to bed, unable to eat or drink, to read or watch TV, or even hold a conversation. I would writhe in agony for hours, unable to escape into sleep.

Once the vomiting and pain started, there was no pain medicine I could take by mouth and keep down. At times, before the advent of Imitrex, my husband would drive and practically carry me into the office of my neurologist for an injection of Demerol. I would get a "floating" sensation and for a few hours, if I lay perfectly still, the vomiting would temporarily subside. But the pain would not leave.

Later, when Imitrex became available, my husband Tony would give me an injection using the long, heavy needle that contained the medication in those days. We would wait and pray for the temporary relief it would bring. Again, the vomiting would subside for a few hours, the pain would become at least bearable, but I would still be unable to eat or drink.

I could only take the recommended dose of Imitrex every 24 hours because of possible dangerous side effects. I would lie in bed and toss and turn and cry and count the hours and minutes before I could take another injection and again get some brief relief.

These migraine attacks began to increase in frequency and intensity. By the spring of 1995, I was experiencing an episode every two weeks, and I was running out of sick days. I was in a job that was both stressful and challenging, dealing with most of the discipline issues in my school. On days when I would have to leave work, I would drive the thirty minutes home alone, in pain, vomiting into a plastic bag on the way. I was too embarrassed to ask anyone to drive me.

When I wasn't in school, my absence meant more work for others on the administrative staff, who had to pick up my responsibilities. I began to feel ashamed of my illness. Particularly since following one of these migraines, I would return to work looking healthy, as if nothing had ever been wrong with me. I blamed myself. Perhaps, if I stuck to a more ascetic diet, ate only fruit and vegetables, drank only water, slept more, exercised more and, of course, prayed and read my Bible more, repented more, maybe this illness would go away. Instead, it got worse.

My illness affected my state of mind as well. I began to fear the onslaught of these attacks. I felt that friends were thinking "Oh, Drenda's having another migraine. Is she really that sick?" My husband and I missed social functions, church and other events. Tony took hikes in the mountains without me on Saturdays and often had to go to other activities we had scheduled by himself. I became depressed and slept less. I lost weight and was chronically tired with dark circles under my eyes.

Tony is a man of great faith. When I met him, I was wandering around in the New Age, believing in Jesus, but not as Messiah and Lord. Tony was my personal John the Baptist, fervent and passionate for Jesus-- all that was lacking was the honey running down the beard and the grasshoppers dangling from his mouth. I credit him with leading me into the relationship I have with the Lord today. In addition, I thank him for being obedient to the voice of God and dragging me into the Randy Clark meeting in 1995 that would change my life.

We first encountered Randy in a little church in Wilmington, North Carolina, in 1994. Tony had heard of Randy's visit to Toronto and the subsequent revival there. When he learned that Randy would be in Wilmington, he immediately made plans for us to go. We live in Kernersville, North Carolina, so the drive would be only a few hours.

When we arrived at the meeting, I was already getting sick. I was not even physically able to go inside. After a couple of hours, I was in such distress that I managed to drag myself into the building to look for Tony. I needed him to give me an injection of Imitrex, since my hand was shaking so badly that I could not do it for myself.

Inside the building, I couldn't believe what I saw. There were bodies everywhere! Some people were laughing, some crying, some rejoicing. People were getting healed, and some were getting delivered. I stepped over people, searching everywhere for Tony. I found him, his head under a chair, sprawled on the floor among all the other bodies. I shook him and begged him to get up and come to the car. I felt I was going to throw up; my head was throbbing, and I was getting desperate. I didn't look for Randy. I knew I couldn't stand up for long and certainly not in line.

I missed the meeting the following day, staying in bed and struggling. We were staying with a couple who belonged to the church where Randy was ministering.

At one point, their youngest child, about three, wandered into my room. I heard her say in her child's voice, "Debil!" I didn't open my eyes, but I heard her speak this one word. She left the room. I knew she had seen in the spirit realm, as young children often do, the source of my illness.

Tony had interceded for me many times. He had done warfare over me and deliverance and prayed repeatedly. On one occasion, when he was commanding the spirit of migraine to leave, I began to feel the sickness and pain suddenly begin to subside. At that moment, we both heard in the center of the room an audible squeal or shriek! We looked at each other in amazement. We knew we had heard the sound of a demon himself in torment from the prayers Tony was praying.

When I was able to return to Randy's meeting, I had some incredible experiences. One of these was a powerful deliverance from witchcraft. I was told later that my fingers hooked into claws and that I had actually tried to scratch at the eyes of my pastor, who was in charge of the deliverance. Randy told my husband that my gums had bled during the intensity of this struggle. Although I experienced a sense of relief and peace after this deliverance, in the days ahead I learned that the migraines had not gone away.

That I was being afflicted by witchcraft made sense to me. My sister and I had always known that, in my family, we "knew" things. Also, as a small child, my sister had cried and talked of seeing a lurid, red devil-like face appear in the corner of her room at times. I had been involved in the New Age as an adult and had visited psychics. One had even volunteered to train me as a psychic because of my "gift." I turned her down.

A year after the Wilmington meeting, I was still struggling to get to work and still battling with illness. A sense of hopelessness set in. When my boss approached me with the recommendation that I take a three-month medical leave, I felt an overwhelming sadness and sense of failure. And anxiety. I sensed there was an unspoken message here. I either had to get well or consider early retirement. At the time, that was not a financial option for me. How was I supposed to get well in three months from an illness that had dogged me for thirty years?

I took the medical leave. I had more tests. Did I have a brain tumor? Despite my doctor's assurances, Tony insisted that no one could have this type of pain without some organic treatable origin. Did I have allergies? More tests. More prayer. More special diets. More rest. Nothing changed.

With only two weeks left of my medical leave, I was growing desperate. I cried out to God. I confessed any sin I could possibly ever have committed and asked for forgiveness. I forgave everyone I thought had ever hurt me. I remember forgiving my grandmother for causing such tension in my parent's marriage. My mother had told me many times how she had interfered in her relationship with my father, the son born late in life and whom she considered her baby.

It was at this time in 1995, with only two weeks of my medical leave left, that we heard that Randy Clark was coming to High Point, North Carolina. He would be holding meetings in a large venue, a former furniture warehouse now rented to the public for special events.

A couple of days before Randy's meeting, Tony and I went to a church in a neighboring city to hear Janelle Wade, a former practicing witch, give her testimony of salvation and deliverance. After years of operating powerfully in the occult, Janelle had gone into ministry. I was fascinated by her story and immediately bought her book.

The morning of the day that Tony and I had planned to go to Randy's meeting in High Point, I began to devour Janelle's book. I couldn't put it down. Tony had left to attend a workshop at the same venue where Randy would be ministering and teaching on healing that evening.

I was standing at the island in our kitchen when I read the last page of Janelle Wade's amazing story. I was suddenly furious! "Why, God, did you do this for her, and yet you won't heal me!" I threw the book across the room. I beat on the counter and told God how angry I was with Him. Why was he deaf to my prayers, and those of my husband and family and friends for me? Why didn't He love me as much as he loved Janelle Wade? I had never done some of things she had done. I sobbed and screamed at God. Why had He abandoned me? What had I done wrong, that I should have to go on suffering like this?

Within minutes, I felt what I had come to call the "veil" begin to fall. This "veil" would bring a sense of heaviness around me and into my body. Pain would attack with blinding intensity. I could feel the oppression and nausea begin. I knew I was in the early stages of another migraine. I dragged myself upstairs and into bed, still sobbing, dreading what I believed the next few days would bring.

I knew I would not be able to go to Randy's meeting. In fact, I didn't want to go at all now. Ironically, I had received the first word of knowledge I had ever had from Randy at the meeting in Wilmington the previous year. This word had brought me tremendous inner healing from abandonment issues associated with the death of my father when I was fourteen. I had received an impartation for the prophetic through Randy that is still my primary and most effective spiritual gift. But on this day, I didn't want to go near a Randy Clark meeting, particularly one focused on healing. What was the point?

At the same time, Tony heard a distinct inner voice during the workshop he was attending in High Point, saying, "Go and get Drenda!" As he was leaving the building to come home, he met a friend who repeated to him, "Tony, you need to go and get Drenda."

Tony arrived home, and when he found me in bed, he told me what had happened. My response was, "I'm not going. I'm too sick to go to this healing meeting. It won't do any good anyway." Tony was insistent that I come, whether through my own volition or by his physically picking me up and carrying me himself. I finally relented, feeling more sick, angry, and resentful than ever.

At the meeting I insisted on sitting in the back row against the wall, feeling ill and miserable. Tony tried to encourage me by saying that Randy might get a word of knowledge about migraines. I replied that if he did, he would have to call out my name, address, and phone number before I went forward. I had been disappointed too many times and felt God had had ample opportunities to heal me if he really wanted to set me free.

About 10:30 p.m., Randy suddenly stopped preaching and announced that God was leading him in another direction. Anyone who had a calling to the healing ministry, he said, was to come forward for prayer. Tony grabbed my hand and said, "That's us. Let's go." I replied that not only did I no longer feel called to the healing ministry, I was sick myself and needed healing. Tony just smiled and led me to the front of the auditorium.

By the time I arrived at the front, I was shaking all over. As Randy prayed from the platform, Fred Gruey, a pastor traveling with Randy, walked by me and touched me gently with two fingers on the forehead and moved on. I was shaking convulsively now. Tony caught me as I fell to the floor.

Within moments I heard a loud and distinct voice inside my head that declared, "We have a right to be here!" I was terrified. My body shook violently, and I writhed from side to side on the floor. In the next three hours, many people came over to pray for me.

A pastor friend of ours asked Tony if he could pray. He had told Tony a few days earlier that while he was in the shower the Lord had told him my illness was rooted in witchcraft. As he was praying, he placed his index finger on my forehead. It felt like a red hot poker going into my skull. I began to manifest even more violently.

Time passed with no change in my condition. A friend of ours said, "We've got to find Randy." When Randy came over, I heard him say gently, "Drenda, we're going to ask Jesus to show us the entry point for these migraines." He prayed softly. Suddenly, I saw myself in my crib. I was one-year-old. My grandmother was standing over me. She was putting the mark of the witch on my forehead. I saw myself in the crib crying and heard myself say, "No, no, don't let her do that to me. Jesus, come and help me!"

I began to weep as I saw in an instant that years of suffering were connected to this moment. Not only migraines, but depression and many of the other struggles in my life had stemmed from this one life-changing experience. Randy said, "Drenda, now you have to forgive your grandmother."

In my anguish and hurt, I told him, "I can't. I can't." The pain and betrayal were too overwhelming. I could only sob. How could she have done this to me? Why? Tony said quietly, "Ask Jesus to help you." Even then, time passed before I was able to utter that simple prayer, to decide that I did want to forgive, to let go the shock and anger I was now feeling towards this woman I had loved so much growing up.

Yet, suddenly, I saw that she had thought she was actually giving me a gift. To her, this was a secret benevolence, not a curse. At that moment, I made the decision in the midst of my tears to utter these simple words, "Jesus, I forgive her. Please, will you forgive her too?" Immediately, Randy took authority over the spirit of migraine and cast it out.

I had the physical sensation of a powerful rush of wind swooshing out of the top of my head. I cannot find words to adequately describe this experience. In a split second, I knew I was free. I cannot describe the lightness, the sense of freedom, the joy, and the ecstasy that followed this moment.

A friend asked Randy if she could anoint me with oil and replace the mark of the witch with the sign of the cross on my forehead. As she did this, I saw myself surrounded by an incredible brilliant white light. There were angelic presences in that light. There was music, powerful but soft, in that light. Jesus Himself was in that light. I remember shouting, "Can you see Him? Can you see Him?" His glory was breathtaking, His presence overwhelming. I did not see His face. I knew Him as the embodiment of Love-- all the love the universe can hold.

When He spoke, He said to me, "I told you that I would come and save you." I knew somehow that even in that crib when I was one-year-old, He was with me. He had made me a promise and He had come to fulfill that promise. He also asked me four questions, each beginning with "Will you…?" Each time with tears I replied, "Yes." Each time, both my hands shot straight up in the air, and I felt His touch as He gave me four different commissions concerning His work in the Kingdom.

I knew I had been healed and set free. I had been delivered out of the throes of torment into a state of ecstasy. My body felt as if electric currents of joy were surging through it and into my heart. I felt freer and lighter than I had ever been.

At 2:00 a.m., Randy told Tony that he would have to get me out of the building. Everyone else had left, and the building had to be locked. Tony scooped me up in his arms and carried me to the car. I was unable to walk or stand, and all night long my body continued to vibrate.

The next morning, I joyfully called my sister to tell her what had happened to me. She told me a strange story. She told me she had been seeing visions of our grandmother all week, with her hair, which she always wore in a bun, hanging down like a witch. She reminded me that our mother had walked into the room when she was one and found my grandmother at the foot of her crib. My sister, two years younger than I, was crying and screaming. She had always loved my grandmother, but after this she began to shy away from her.

I cannot explain all that I have just related here or answer all the questions that my testimony may raise for the reader. When the Pharisees questioned the man blind from birth to whom Jesus gave sight, he was not able to give an answer to all their inquiries. His reply was simply, "One thing I know, that though I was blind now I see" (John 9:25). My testimony is like that. All I really know is that Jesus has set me free.

Not since that day in 1995 when Randy prayed for me, have I endured another demonic migraine attack. I still thank Jesus regularly for my deliverance. It is not easy to write my story, and the memories of those attacks are difficult to revisit or think about. The memories are repulsive: the excruciating pain, the nausea, the smells, the sensitivity to light and touch, the sense of my entire being racked with a demonic presence that I and others felt helpless to drive away can still be overwhelming.

In 1999, I was able to retire from the school system after a thirty-year career, at a date of my own choosing. My husband and I are still enjoying my freedom. I no longer wake up to the oppression and fear I lived with for so many years, wondering if I will spend another weekend sick in bed. Daily life is not shadowed by the dread that my husband and I will have to back out of engagements or family holidays at the last minute because I have had another debilitating migraine attack.

I realize that I lost so many days of my life unable to work, daily tasks, or enjoy simple pleasures because of an assignment against me from the enemy. Now God is redeeming those days.

My husband and I are grateful to God that he spoke so clearly to Tony to get me to Randy's meeting in 1995. We are grateful to Randy for his faithfulness as an obedient servant of Christ. Most of all, we are grateful to Jesus, who always keeps His promises.

Carter Wood
Anointed, Activated, and Commissioned

All who enter into relationship with Christ find the journey full of ebbs and flows that direct their course and secure their destiny. King David wrote in Psalms 37:23, "The steps of a man are established by the Lord, and He delights in his way."[2] It is God's pleasure to see us succeed as we advance the Kingdom together with Him on the earth. In turn, it is the believer's passionate desire to "declare His strength to this generation"[3] and see "the knowledge of the glory of the Lord fill the earth as the water covers the sea."[4] It is in this mutual love affair between God and man that we find our worth and purpose on the earth.

It is abundantly clear that it is "from glory to glory'" He is changing us.[5] We were born to be carriers of God's glory, but the passageway to that glory is called "change." As we review the history of our lives, it is easy to have conversations about the "woulda-coulda-shoulda" regrets of life. Likewise, others have been paralyzed while

---

[2] NASB

[3] Psalms 71:18 (NASB)

[4] Habakkuk 2:14 (NASB)

[5] 2 Corinthians 3:18 (NASB)

camping out by the smoldering embers of yesterday's victories. We must learn to walk through the failures of our past, without letting them define us. It is necessary to rehearse our victories, making them the springboard to Kingdom greatness.

David told King Saul, "Your servant has killed both lion and bear; and this uncircumcised Philistine will be like one of them..."[6] David started with lions and bears, moved to giants, and then conquered nations. David became a hero when he defeated Goliath, but he became a champion when winning battles became a lifestyle. Your history alone cannot determine your future. However, as you agree with your history, you empower it. You need not condescend or think lightly of your past to bring value to the present and hope for what lies ahead. Our beginnings are God-given and become the building blocks of greater and deeper realities of the Kingdom of God. Our starting places are glorious, and through every stage we move to greater revelation, manifesting His goodness to a generation that desperately needs Him.

No one reaches their destiny by themselves. The Apostle Paul tells us, "There are many people around who can't wait to tell you what you've done wrong, but there aren't many fathers willing to take the time and effort to help you grow up."[7] As the Church is maturing, she is beginning to gather around spiritual fathers. Fathers are those people who have the unique ability to bring identity and value to young lives. As it is true in the natural, it is also true in the spiritual. There are many saints who have been spiritually orphaned, many who are now finding hope in true spiritual fathers.

I am grateful to all those who have poured into my life through the years, giving me opportunity to grow and room to fail. These men and women have instilled into me the faith, confidence, and

---

[6] 1 Samuel 17:36 (NKJV)

[7] 1 Corinthians 4:15 (TMSG)

courage necessary to succeed. Randy Clark is one of those on my personal list of people who have filled the role of spiritual father in my life. I am thankful beyond words to him and the Global Awakening family for their contributions, as they are, "equipping the saints for the work of ministry."[8] I have been touched. I have been changed, and it is glorious!

I was raised in a Christian home and in an Assemblies of God church that started before in my grandparents' front room I was born. From my childhood, I remember a church life that included strong sermons and altars filled with people seeking God. I would spend time at the altar every Sunday evening, crying out to God and soaking in His presence. I had my prayer spot, down front on the left-hand side. It was there, on the end of the upholstered altar bench, that I would routinely bury my head in my arms, asking God to use me. I can still hear in my mind the piano and organ music playing as Sister Merrill, our pastor's wife and choir director, sang old hymns and popular Gaither songs that moved me into deep places of prayer and intimacy with God. It did not seem extraordinary at the time, but looking back, I now see the foundation those times laid.

It was at the ripe old age of three-and-a half years when I first encountered God. Even now, my memories of that amazing time are as clear as the day it happened. There was a guest speaker at church that October evening. Sister Hookie was a fiery evangelist who came often to our church. I do not know what she preached, and at such a young age, I did not understand or even care. I was sitting contently in my father's lap playing with his fingers and sucking on a LifeSaver®. Those were the days of learning to sit quietly in church.

At the end of her message, Sister Hookie had everyone stand and gave an appeal to those who needed to "get saved" or wanted to be filled with the Holy Spirit. No one responded. She again began to

---

[8] Ephesians 4:12 (NKJV)

encourage the congregation to move from their pews and come to the altar. Still no one moved. There was an awkward stillness in the room. That is when I began to tremble in my father's arms. Tears were flowing down my cheeks. There was obviously something happening to me, so my dad whispered in my ear, asking me if there was anything wrong. I answered with a stammering, "No." He then asked, "Carter, do you want to go down to the altar?" Through my tears I said yes. My dad told me that if this was something God was doing, then I needed to walk to the front on my own. A big task for a three-year-old. So my dad lowered me to the ground, and when my feet hit the floor, I ran as fast as my little legs could take me. I found "my spot" at the altar for the first time and began to pray. I was there with no coaching, and I gave my life to Jesus.

It was not too long before I felt an adult's hands under my arms, picking me up. It was Sister Hookie holding me close as she walked up to the platform. I looked from the platform to the congregation packed wall to wall. Every eye was watching to see what would happen. Finding a microphone, she interviewed me: "Did you ask Jesus into your heart?" Through a tearful voice I responded, "Yes, Jesus is in my heart." She continued, "Did Jesus take away your sins?" "Uh huh!" That's "yes" in three-year-old speech. You could feel the spiritual tension begin to rise in the room. "Carter," she asked, "Are there others in this room who need to find Jesus?" There was a heavenly courage that was now on me that was more mature than a three-year-old would normally possess. I looked at the congregation and said, "Jesus wants to know everyone. We need to know Jesus!" With those words, saints and sinners alike began to run to the front. The Holy Spirit came in power that night.

I grew up the son of a carpenter. Hmm, sounds like someone I know. Together with my two siblings, my grandparents, and my recently divorced father, we lived in a country house on a few acres with several outbuildings. One of those buildings served as the shop where my father built cabinets and furniture for a living. It was there I spent much of my time, playing as any eight-year-old boy might do. I loved to make boxes, swords, and other props that would aid my imagination in taking me to far-away, make-believe places. It was a young boy's delight, and I would play there for hours at a time on the sawdust mountains in a world of towering lumber.

One day after school, I ran into the shop to greet my father. I remember watching him pick up a large sheet of plywood and place it on the table saw as he skillfully ripped it into long strips. It seemed he was always covered from head to toe in sawdust. He looked up and acknowledged me with a welcoming smile as he turned off the saw. I ran as fast as I could and took a full-on flying leap into his outstretched arms. He caught me in midair and held me tight. I can still remember the feeling of the rough sawdust on his face as he pressed his cheek against mine.

I turned and saw my grandfather come into the shop to do a few chores. It was a cold winter day, and he began building a fire in a homemade stove made out of a fifty-gallon steel drum. As I was watching him stoke the flame, he picked up a scrap of hardwood and broke it over his knee. That very instant a twelve-inch piece of wood splintered off and lodged in my left eye on a horizontal plane. The pain was excruciating. It was as though I had been stung by a giant hornet.

I instinctively reached up and pulled the stick out of my eye. I ran as fast as I could into the house to look into the bathroom mirror. I took my fingers and pried open my eye to see what damage had been done. There was a gaping hole where the pointed stick had once been. My dad ran in close behind me and asked to look. Without a word, he hurriedly left the room and called the doctor for advice. The doctor told my dad to bypass the emergency room at the hospital and come straight to his office as soon as possible.

My grandfather ran to the car and jumped into the driver's seat while my dad scooped me into his arms and laid me in his lap in the back seat. I could feel my body trembling uncontrollably as I went into shock. The touch of my father's hand stroking my forehead was a welcomed and reassuring comfort, but the pain of the injury and the fear of what this all meant was intense. My dad leaned over close to my ear and asked, "Carter, do you want to pray?" I answered, "Yes, Daddy, please pray for me." To this day I remember the simplicity of his prayer, "God, Carter loves you. He needs a touch from you. Don't let him go through life with a blind eye. Heal his eye in Jesus' name." I immediately stopped shaking and settled down as we made our way through town to the doctor.

When we arrived, the doctor and his staff were waiting for us. They rushed us into the small examination room, and the doctor immediately sat me down in front of a microscope and began examining my eye. We were listening closely for any verbal clue the doctor might give to the condition of my eye. All we heard for several minutes were, "wows" and "hmms," with the occasional "This is remarkable," and "I have never seen this before."

I was not comforted. Eight-year-old boys do not want to be seen as "different." The doctor leaned back from his work and asked, "What did you say happened to Carter's eye?" My dad repeated the story of the stick, the hole in the eye, and the prayer. The doctor said, "Leroy, come over here and look at Carter's eye through this microscope." How I wish I could have been on the other side of the scope. My dad asked, "What am I looking at? All I can see is a group of things moving around." The doctor answered, "What you are seeing is the eye being healed. The eye is being knit together at an accelerated rate. We are watching a miracle take place." Except for a little bruising in my eye, I left the office that day totally healed.

Nearly four decades after that miracle, in May 2003, I experienced one of the greatest shifts in my life and ministry. My wife Diana and I had been in ministry for more than twenty years. While there were victories and spiritual growth during these years, we reached a turning point that would forever change our lives.

This particular Sunday morning was quite typical. The worship team was in high gear, singing songs of praise and celebration. Passionate voices filled the auditorium with declarations to a loving and faithful God. The presence of God was tangible in the air, and people were responding to a gentle move of the Holy Spirit. I stepped up to the pulpit and began speaking from the chosen text that day in Mark 16, declaring, "These signs will accompany those who have believed...in the name of Jesus, we will cast out demons...we will lay hands on the sick, and they will recover."[9] That morning the word of the Lord was exceptionally strong. The response in the room was one of enthusiastic embrace. The altars were filled as hungry people cried out to God for more.

As I prayed for those at the altar that day, I heard the Holy Spirit speak to me, saying, "Carter, what about you? How are you going to respond to your own message?" I learned a long time ago that God does not ask questions because He does not know the answers. The question pricked my heart. "What do you mean, what about me?" After all, I had a good ministry. The church was growing and strong. Furthermore, I was often in the nations preaching the Gospel. But I was not getting away with my excuse, because deep inside I knew what the Holy Spirit was after. I had been found out. It was time to stop hiding behind my comfort zone of vocational ministry and personally believe. These signs will follow Carter because he believes.

I wasted no time and began to seek the Lord regarding this newfound revelation. It was not too many days later that Diana and I

---

[9] The Great Commission, Mark 16:15–18 (NASB)

visited Bethel Church in Redding, California. It was there, as Pastor Bill Johnson was speaking, that we heard Randy Clark's name for the first time. He spoke passionately about the profound affect Randy had had on his life and encouraged everyone to participate with Randy by going on one of his international trips.

As Pastor Bill was talking, I heard the Holy Spirit say to me, "Go! Not one time, but five." So I took that direction from the Lord and set out to make plans to do just that. It was nearly six months before we could go on our first Global Awakening trip. In the meantime, we bought tickets, packed our bags, and headed off to Toronto, Canada.

In October 2003, we attended the ten-year anniversary of the Toronto Blessing Revival. Everyone's expectations were high. There were many who were obviously "veterans" in the renewal movement, but there were still others in the room like me who had all the signs of being newbies. I was both excited and apprehensive about what I would experience. One thing was for sure: I had to have more of God and was willing to go to any length to find Him.

That night Randy Clark was scheduled to preach, and preach he did. In his opening remarks, he asked all the church leaders in the room to come down to the front and stand. My wife Diana and I got as close to the platform as we could and stopped in an aisle behind the already-packed altar area. After a few minutes, Randy had us sit down on the floor, and he began his message. He started by declaring, "Everyone here tonight will receive an impartation from the Holy Spirit, but there will be some who will receive a commission from the Lord." As I heard these words, I felt the fire of the Holy Spirit begin to burn in my chest. Visions of what this could mean began to swirl through my spirit. Could this be a time that God would set His Spirit upon my life in greater measure? With every word out of Randy's mouth, my heart burned more intensely. Any fear and apprehension I had before that moment was now replaced by the wooing of the Holy Spirit. The unseeable spiritual activity in the room was growing stronger every second. My spirit began to resound with expectation. I felt as though I was the only one in the room. As each word left Randy's mouth, it found its destination in the bulls-eye of my heart. I was undone.

About the time I felt I could take no more, Randy closed his message and began to pray for leaders. From the platform he was laying his hands on the heads of those who had lined up in front of him. He would pray for one row, and then those behind would move up to form another line. About forty-five minutes later, it was finally our turn for prayer. I stepped up in front of the platform, determined to receive all God had for me. I could hear Randy's prayers as he moved down the line towards me. I silently asked myself, "How does a person prepare and posture himself for a moment like this?" I heard the voice of the Holy Spirit answer, "Posture yourself in faith and do not be passive." Have you ever asked a question only to receive an answer that raised more questions than you started with?

Almost before I had time to reflect, I heard Randy praying for my wife Diana, "More of you, Holy Spirit." I was next in line and uttered a quick prayer, "God, I want all you have for me!" As Randy laid his hands on my head, I felt the power of God surge through my body. Before I could think about what I was doing, I grabbed his wrists. When I did, the power of God came through my body with what felt like 10,000 volts of electricity. About every ten seconds, I would feel another surge of power as though someone flipped a switch. I lay on the floor a long time feeling the wonderfully painful surges of the Holy Spirit course through my body. This continued through the night and into the next day. To this day, merely remembering this encounter brings the manifest presence of God on my life.

Remembering those who traveled with me, I pulled myself together the best I could and crawled to where they were sitting. I must have been quite a sight because everyone erupted in laughter as I approached. One of the "veterans" of the house passed by, looked at me and said, "Yup, you got it!" Whether I received an anointing or commission that day, heaven knows and history will tell, but the life-altering effects of that outpouring and infilling of the Holy Spirit started immediately.

There was a marked increase of anointing and healings after we returned home from Toronto, but our new season of ministry was really launched in Sao Paulo, Brazil, in April 2004. It had been several years since I traveled in the nations, and I was carrying some battle scars of days gone by. Diana had received a word while at Bethel in Redding, California, "God is going to do it again, but it will not hurt this time." My faith was growing and overriding my concerns, and I sensed an invitation of the Holy Spirit to go deeper.

We arrived in Sao Paulo, settled into our room, and quickly rushed to the meeting that was gathering in the hotel conference room for orientation and prayer. As I would soon find out, impartation, not information, was the primary objective. Testimony after testimony came forth. My faith was being built up with every story of victory. Randy and the Global Awakening team began to pray for everyone in the room.

When Randy started praying for Diana, he began to prophesy over her and the team we brought with us. What we did not know until later was the prophecy he spoke over us that night was the same one spoken over him just before he was used when the Holy Spirit fell in Toronto. "Test Me now, test Me now. Don't be afraid. I will back you up! I want your eyes to be opened to see my resources in the heavenlies for you, just as Elisha prayed for Gehazi's eyes to be opened. And do not become anxious, because when you become anxious, you can't hear Me." For us, there was no historical context for what was prophesied, but we took it as from the Lord. I believe to this day that it is still unfolding in our lives.

The next morning we arrived at the venue where leaders were gathering to be trained. Mike Kaylor was teaching the Five-Step Prayer Model that morning. At the end of the teaching, the Global team was asked to come to the front to pray for the sick. I remembered the fear and insecurity that welled up in me. I thought, "No, it could not be that matter-of-fact. I do not know how to do this."

I quickly collected my thoughts and began rehearsing the events that had brought me to this very place, remembering what the Holy Spirit spoke to me about a year earlier: "Carter, what about you? How are you going to respond to your own message?" Here I was responding to the challenge of the Holy Spirit. This was my spiritual D-day on the metaphorical beaches of my personal Normandy. I was scared, but losing this spiritual battle was not an option. I must believe. I must pray. I must heal the sick in Jesus' name. I can recall but a few of the specifics of those I prayed for and the outcome of those prayers; the spiritual breakthrough that morning was paramount.

After lunch and a time of rest in the afternoon, we arrived at the evening meeting. The atmosphere was charged with the presence of the Holy Spirit. You could feel the faith and expectation from those who had gathered for healing oozing from their spiritual pores. That night, healing broke out everywhere, first from the ministry team giving words of knowledge and then again after Randy's message.

When we were released to pray for the sick, a man walked up to me who was in his mid-forties, suffering with constant back pain from an injury five years earlier. I placed my hand on his back and prayed, asking the Holy Spirit to come. I asked if he felt anything, and he responded, saying he felt heat around the injury. I was encouraged. I instructed the interpreter, "Tell him, heat is good." I continued to pray and commanded his back to be healed, in Jesus name! Again, I directed the interpreter, "Ask him if he is feeling anything." After his answer to her, she said to me, "He said the pain is all gone." "Do something you could not do before," I said with an excitement in my voice. He began bending down to touch his toes. He looked up at me with eyes that said, "I have no pain, and look at me, I have not been able to do this for a long time." He continued to exercise his miracle with twisting and turning as he smiled from ear-to-ear. We both began to praise God together, him for his healing and me because I was being fascinated by God's goodness. His word is true. His mercy everlasting! That night many of the people who received prayer were healed.

After praying for a dozen or more people, I felt compelled to go watch Randy. In an attempt to stay inconspicuous, I stood back a few yards from where he was praying. I watched and prayed for about ten minutes, when Randy looked up at me and motioned me over to help him pray for people. It was there for the next hour or so that I was immersed in the tutelage of a man of God. Occasionally he would say, "Look what is happening right now," or "Watch what happens when I pray this way." I was amazed by the spiritual wisdom and compassion with which he ministered. After more than an hour of ministry, he leaned over and began telling me of an invitation he received from one of his spiritual mentors to come and follow him as he ministered. "Carter," he said, "I want to give you a similar invitation while you are here." From that moment on, I knew I had the liberty to watch, learn, and grow.

As the outreach unfolded, I was changing. Hope was filling my heart, and I was not alone. It seemed everyone on the team had entered into a realm of signs, wonders, and miracles. They were homemakers, business people, white- and blue-collar workers, young and old. People from all backgrounds were being used mightily by God.

They were ministering in ways that were historically reserved for the highly trained and gifted vocational ministers. Their testimonies were nothing short of amazing and ranged from muscle pain and skin conditions being healed to tumors disappearing, demons cast out, and the blind seeing.

We were all stepping into the destiny purpose that was characteristic of the early church. The joy of the Lord could be seen on every life. "This is why I was created" was frequently heard. Many of the paradigms and ideals of my past were being shaken, and my mind was being renewed in this Kingdom culture of liberty, grace, and power.

When Diana and I returned home, we both commented on how much emotional and spiritual healing had taken place in us on the trip. We had been touched by God and changed. A fundamental shift had come to our lives and subsequently to our church. The question the Holy Spirit asked me, about how I was going to respond to my own message, was now finding greater meaning in life and ministry.

With all of the experiences of impartation and miracles in recent months, I was now provoked to consider the church I was pastoring. It wasn't what we were doing, it was what we were not doing that needed to change. It now became important to us to create an environment where every person is valued and reassured of their personal destiny. Additionally, we understood in a new way that every believer must be given opportunities to encounter God and be equipped for the work of ministry with signs and wonders following. For us, this is the normal way of living and right in line with our human design. Life is now a lab.

Four months later I sent this email.

Hello Randy,

I felt compelled to write you regarding the things that God is doing in Santa Rosa since my wife Diana and I returned from Brazil last April. There has been a remarkable stepping up in the anointing since our return and a general healing anointing being released in the church. It seems that the whole congregation has entered into doing the works that Jesus did. I want to share two short testimonies with you.

Last April in Brazil, you asked me to take the beginning of a service, that you were going to arrive late and you suggested that I not pray for the sick, but have the team do words of knowledge and then encourage the congregation enter into "high praise" and declare Psalms 103. When we did, about 90 percent of the 120 or so people that were standing were healed. Three weeks later after returning to Santa Rosa, I was in our Sunday morning worship service and felt the Holy Spirit's leading to do it again there. When we did, the Holy Spirit began to move powerfully in the room. There were about 20 or so people healed, several with long term problems. Praise God!

Then again last Sunday morning after words of knowledge were given, we had the congregation gather around those who were standing and pray for them. Twenty-six people were healed, nearly everyone who was standing.

There has been a shift in our church. Very seldom is there not someone healed in our corporate gatherings. Randy, thank you for investing in our lives and being faithful to your call.

Diana and I took a second trip to Brazil with Global Awakening in December 2004. Considering our last experience, we had high expectations for what God would do. We arrived at the hotel in Vitoria and got settled in.

We loaded the buses and continued to the venue where people were gathering to hear Randy and to receive ministry from the Global team. We were encouraged by the Global leaders to spend some time in prayer for the meetings as we traveled. I looked out the window and began to pray. I thought I recognized a building as we passed by, but quickly dismissed it as being just a coincidence of similarity. I continued to pray. As more of the scenery passed by, I began to realize I had been in this exact place before. How could this be? I had never been in Vitoria, Brazil before. Then I remembered- I had seen this place in a dream I had four years earlier. It was not a dream that I had ever written down, but one of those forgotten before waking up. Here I was, remembering with total recall every detail. Signs and wonders indeed!

In the dream, an angel of the Lord took me high above the earth. As we flew over and through cities, I would see a city ignite and begin to burn. We would go a little further and see another city set on fire. This happened five times in the dream. I asked the angel what these things meant. He began to explain that God was getting ready to ignite five capital cities with the fire of the Holy Spirit. These cities would be a source of fiery testimony and impartation in their region, as "a city set on a hill cannot be hid." As I came back from these deep thoughts, I found tears running down my face. Thoughts of intense wonder filled my heart. What did this mean to the city of Vitoria, Brazil? I concluded that if I was properly discerning the dream, then two things are abundantly clear. First, Vitoria is a capital city. Second, this city is slated for a great move of God.

When we arrived at the venue, I immediately set out to get information to confirm my thesis. "Is Vitoria, Brazil a capital city?" I asked several Global Awakening team members, but none knew the answer. I moved on, looking for a Brazilian who spoke English. After several failed attempts, I found a translator working with our team who spoke English. "I have a question for you, and please forgive my ignorance. Tell me, is Vitoria a capital city?" "Yes," he answered. "Vitoria is the capital city of the state of Espirito Santo." My spirit leaped within me. I understood very little Portuguese but I knew enough to translate this. "Vitoria" means "victory" and "Espirito Santo" means "Holy Spirit."

I declared out loud, "We have come to minister in the city of Victory located in the state of the Holy Spirit! Victory is in the Holy Spirit!" The prophetic significance of this revelation, combined with remembering the dream, was sounding an alarm in my spirit that was undeniable. My expectations were now somewhere out in the stratosphere. What could it mean, and how should I proceed? The evening ministry time began, and words of knowledge were given. Randy preached, and people were saved, healed, and delivered. All the while, I continued to contemplate this amazing moment.

Diana and I crawled into bed about midnight that night. I think we set a world speed record for the fastest time for any couple to fall asleep. We were told at the beginning of the trip that we would get two naps a day, one in the afternoon and one at night. They were not teasing. About one o'clock in the morning, I awoke with Diana shaking me and saying there was a knock at our door. I quickly made my way across the dark room, guided by the light seeping under the door from the hallway. I opened the door slightly and peeked out. "Oh, hi Randy," I said. "What can I do for you?" He answered, "I wanted to see if you would be interested in sharing a morning teaching session with a Vineyard pastor this morning?" I said I would be honored. After a short time of questions and answers, I closed the door and went back to sleep.

I rose early to prepare and pray for my assignment, ate a quick breakfast, and set off with the team for the morning ministry training time. When we arrived, the church was filled with about 300 people. It was a warm, humid day, and the air was still. The Vineyard pastor finished his amazing teaching, and then it was my turn. I made my way to the front and placed my notes on the pulpit. Looking at the congregation, I said, "I feel that I am to forego my teaching this morning." When I said this, a wind came through the auditorium and blew my notes off the podium. The congregation gasped. The presence of God immediately filled the room. Without saying a word, many began to raise their hands and worship God. The increase of spiritual activity was undeniable.

I began by giving testimony of my ride on the bus and the revealed dream of five revival cities. I explained that if Vitoria was to be one of those cities, then there would be those who would answer the call of God. As I was speaking, a cloud of God's glory entered through the back door and hung over the entire congregation, six to seven feet above the floor. This was one of the few times in my life I could see the unseen activity of the supernatural. I declared, "The manifest presence of God is in the room. It is time for those who feel they are to say 'Yes' to God to stand to their feet." At least half the congregation stood.

The glory cloud was now hovering just inches over their heads. I asked everyone to close their eyes, raise their hands, and begin to pray. I was quite curious about what would happen if someone touched the cloud. As they raised their hands, they pierced the membrane of the cloud. Immediately, many fell to the ground shaking violently. Others began to speak in tongues, and some began to jump and dance. The volume in the room was intense. The meeting was now totally out of our control.

The Global Awakening team was looking to me for instruction, so I yelled, "Go pray for people!" They went out into the congregation and began to lay their hands on people and pray. That day most, if not all of those we prayed for were healed and filled with the Holy Spirit. What a move of God!

Again, I was traveling from the United States to Brazil for another Global trip. I was staring outside the window of the plane quietly praying when I heard the voice of the Holy Spirit speak to me. He began to remind me of my eye being healed and the details pertaining to it. He said, "You have authority in the territory of your breakthrough." As I meditated on this word, I felt my spirit leap. I heard in my heart, "Every word from God comes with an invitation." I was to begin to pray for blind eyes to be opened.

Before this, no one that I had prayed for had received their sight as a result of prayer. However, on this trip, people began coming to me with an unusual frequency, needing prayer for their eyes. It is noteworthy that many of them had problems with their left eye. Let me just remind you that it was my left eye that was healed when I was a boy.

I am sure I prayed for more than twenty people with eye issues on that particular trip. In one of the first mornings of ministry after the message, the team was praying for those who needed healing. I was praying for a man who was blind in his left eye. After fifteen to twenty minutes of no improvement, I leaned over to Randy, who was near me, and asked, "Why are blind eyes not being healed?" He answered, "Because that is not what God is doing right now." Hmm. That was not the answer I was expecting, but it seemed to have a deeper meaning than what appeared on the surface. I went back to praying for this man, but did not see him healed.

The evening meeting started off with powerful worship and a dynamic word from Randy. While I was praying for people at the end of the service, a teenager ran up to me and urged me to come pray for a blind woman. I agreed and followed her to an elderly woman sitting in a wheelchair. Through an interpreter, I learned that she had been blind for more than twenty years. A cataract on her left eye limited her to seeing only bright lights and the dim movement of shadows. She lost the sight in her other eye during a surgical procedure that severed the optic nerve. I was deeply moved with compassion for the woman. She needed a creative miracle.

I began to pray, checking in every few minutes for any signs of improvement. Nothing seemed to work. The minutes turned into nearly an hour. Fatigue was setting in, and my faith was beginning to wane. I took a deep breath and cried out from a deep place inside me. All of a sudden I was no longer in the room. I cannot perfectly explain what happened, but I found myself standing before Jesus, pleading this blind woman's case. "Jesus, You said that those who believed in You would do the works You did. I have believed in You my entire life. You healed my left eye. I know You can do it again. You promised to do whatever I asked in Your name. This woman needs a miracle, and I am asking You to restore her eyesight." I immediately found myself in front of this woman again. Without missing a beat I declared, "IN JESUS' NAME!" I tested her again, putting my fingers in front of her eyes, moving them back and forth. She was seeing about fifty-percent better. We continued to pray and, within moments, her eyesight was completely restored.

The woman looked across the room, recognizing her son whom she had not seen for nearly twenty years. With excitement in her voice she said, "That is my son. He looks older than I remember, but that is him." With that said, she motioned for him to come to her, and they engaged in a long and emotional "visual" reunion. She put her hands on each side of his face and looked into his eyes with eyes that said, "I thought I would never see you again." Hugs, kisses, and tears went on for what seemed like forever. It was the celebration of the Kingdom in power.

They spoke together for a few minutes in Portuguese as if they were getting reacquainted, and then she turned and looked into my eyes, asking in a playful sort of way, "Do you want to know what I am looking forward to the most?" I nodded. "Tomorrow I will read the newspaper for the first time in twenty years." I celebrated with her, knowing that this was a bigger event than I had the ability to comprehend. With that, I gave her a hug and made my way to the bus, amazed beyond words at what had just happened.

The angel who visited Daniel declared, "the people who know their God shall be strong, and carry out great exploits."[10] It is sheer delight to know Him and be used by Him. My passion is to go on to greater depths in Him and take as many others with me as possible. God's people are arising and beginning to understand the reason they were created.

One morning while I was praying, I saw a vision of a child's playground in the middle of a large green field. When I approached the arched entrance, I could read the name of the park, *"The World's Impossibilities."* The park was full of the toys you would typically find, such as swings, slides, and metal bars to climb on. As I walked around the grounds, I observed people wandering through the equipment as if they had no knowledge of what to do at a park like this. Still others could be seen huddled together in fear and intimidation. Then there were those who were content sitting on a bench watching others play. My attention was quickly drawn away by the playful laughter of those who were enjoying swinging, climbing, and jumping on the toys. This is when I heard the Holy Spirit say, *"The World's Impossibilities* are the playground of the believer."

We were created to participate in the plans of God on the earth and be fascinated while doing it. Jesus said, "...with God all things

---

[10] Daniel 11:32 (NKJV)

are possible."[11] God is raising up champions on the earth who will not consider impossibilities the final word, those who long for His glory and declare His Kingdom. All of this starts with just one moment. He spoke through the prophets of old about a generation that He would pour His Spirit upon a generation who would walk in power, saying, "And afterward, I will pour out my Spirit on all people. Your sons and daughters will prophesy, your old men will dream dreams, your young men will see visions. Even on my servants, both men and women, I will pour out my Spirit in those days."[12]

We are that generation, longing to be Changed in a Moment-again!

---

11   Matthew 19:26 (NKJV)
12   Joel 2:28-29 (NIV)

Mark Anderson
Empowered for Evangelism in India

I greatly admire Randy Clark because he walks in humility and believes strongly in team ministry. As a result of this humble attitude, God has used him to spread revival all over the world. Millions have come into the Kingdom of God as those he has prayed over have taken the Gospel to the far reaches of the world. I first saw Randy Clark and Bill Johnson minister in Castle Rock, Colorado, in August 2007. That week there were more than 1,000 testimonies of healings and miracles that took place through the living Christ. Many phenomenal signs and wonders occurred that week.

Roland and Heidi Baker (Iris Ministries) are just one example of the results of impartation through Randy's ministry. Since Randy prayed over them in Toronto, they have planted many thousands of churches in Africa. Undeniable miracles, signs, and wonders have taken place, and many have been raised from the dead through their ministry. To be honest with you, as a missionary evangelist, I wanted in on that anointing to reach more people with the Gospel of Jesus Christ.

I have been in ministry for more than 30 years. We have traveled all over the world to many nations, conducting evangelistic campaigns and leadership conferences, and performing rock 'n roll as an evangelistic tool. We have witnessed the Lord doing many undeniable miracles along with signs and wonders. My wife Sharmila and I try to remain hungry for more so we can be more effective as we travel to spread the Gospel of Jesus Christ. This is what led me to Castle Rock, Colorado to attend the Randy Clark and Bill Johnson conference. During that conference Randy prayed an impartation over me. I felt nothing, but received the impartation by faith, knowing something good would happen afterwards.

Would you like to experience Jesus in a much more powerful and meaningful way? You can.

Soon after, my daughter and her friend saw an angel in our house as we were preparing for our October 2007 campaign in Moradabad, Uttar Pradesh, India. Sharmila and I were crying out for a greater measure of His manifested presence in our lives and ministry. We all need to be humble enough to recognize times of spiritual stagnation in our lives and ask God for a fresh and greater experience with Christ if we are to see a true move of God with greater miracles, signs, and wonders.

Moradabad is a city with a predominantly Muslim population that has been a hotbed of Hindu and Muslim clashes. Nobody had ever conducted a city-wide, open-air campaign there before. Many pastors and churches in Moradabad had low expectations when we arrived, but later repented for that attitude.

Before we left for Moradabad, I told Sharmila that I sensed that this trip would be a turning point in our ministry in North India and that we would experience a breakthrough on this trip. We had already been witnessing Christ doing many miracles in India, but we sensed He would increase the intensity.

During our Moradabad campaign, many people who were healed testified of either seeing, hearing, or being touched by Jesus. Even though we had seen the living Christ healing thousands in India, never before had so many people testified of seeing, hearing, or feeling Jesus touch them. Some felt His hand caress them. Others experienced a current flow through their bodies as they fell to the ground, healed or radically changed.

During our five-day city-wide, open air campaign, approximately 11,500 people (mostly Muslim) decided to become Jesus' followers by surrendering to His Lordship. Many hundreds were healed of all kinds of ailments. Most people who testified they were healed said they either audibly heard Jesus' voice, saw a vision of Him, or saw angels. One gentleman said he saw thousands of angels all over the campaign grounds.

The first night there were about 2,000 in attendance, but by the final night more than 9,000 people had gathered, hungry to hear the Word of God. Just a few of the healings from that campaign included:

> **Mukesh Kumar** who testified that during the mass prayer for healing he told Jesus, "If you are real, I want to experience you." Immediately he felt warmth in his body, followed by coolness. Then a strong current went through him, and he fell to the ground. He arose knowing that Jesus was the true God and decided to follow Him.
>
> **Momine**, a young Muslim boy had no blood circulation on one side of his face, leaving him unable to blink his eye. The Lord touched him, and he was able to blink his eye and speak clearly.
>
> **Vandana**, who suffered with seizures and asthma, sat alone at the far end of the grounds. During the mass

prayer, Jesus appeared to her and told her that she was healed.

Sunil Massih saw Jesus in the midst of the crowd along with thousands of angels. He said that one of the angels touched him.

Vineet Kumar, 12 years old, had severe pain in his lungs. He testified that someone touched him, and he heard an audible voice say to him, "Son, you are healed! Go up and testify." This young boy was extremely charged. He began to boldly praise Jesus in front of the huge crowd.

Neelam, a young girl, saw Jesus appear in her bedroom. She was bed ridden with jaundice (swollen liver). Jesus audibly told her to go to the campaign, where she would be healed. Despite being bedridden, she came to the campaign, carried by her family, and was instantly healed by Jesus.

At these meetings, the blind saw, the deaf heard, cripples danced for joy, tumors dissolved, the demonized were set free, and individuals on their death beds received healing. The power of God was present to heal in a mighty way. Many people testified that they literally felt a presence reach into their bodies and pull the sickness out of them.

News of the campaign spread to surrounding towns, and by the final night people had come from great distances to receive healing from Christ. The local television station covered the campaign, which was good publicity for us. Articles about the campaign and the healings along with my message appeared in newspapers as well.

We heard that on the Sunday after the campaign every church

added at least five or six new families. Healing testimonies continued to flow in. The pastors pledged to disciple all the souls harvested during this campaign. We purchased New Testaments for those who came to Christ. People in Moradabad were saying that the true God really visited their town and shook it.

During the campaign, one young man was so convicted of his sin and the importance of following Jesus that he went to the government to obtain permission to be baptized (In many parts of North India, one needs the government's permission to be baptized as a Christian, if converting from another religion).

We also ministered in a special healing service and youth concert for the New Life Churches in Gurgoan, a suburb of New Delhi. Many turned to Christ, and many testified of being healed by Him. Even after we left, the miracles continued. Sharmila's mother, India campaign coordinator Renuka Frank, has said we have enough invitations in India now to keep us busy for the next ten years.

We are continuing to see Jesus move powerfully in each campaign we conduct in India, despite opposition. Since that October 2007 trip, we have witnessed Jesus doing wonderful miracles in our India outreaches. When we humbled ourselves, received an impartation from one of God's modern-day generals and came to Jesus for more, He took our ministry to another level in India.

In the two years since Randy prayed for us, we have seen close to 35,000 people come to Christ in our North India campaigns alone. Most of the areas where we conduct our outreaches are unreached, and there is strong, militant Hindu activity. We've seen more miracles, more appearances of Jesus and angels to the lost, and greater manifestations of His presence. We realize there are other giftings in the Body of Christ that can help us be more effective. We are grateful for Randy Clark and Bill Johnson's influence which has increased the fruit of our ministry.

With our daughter seeing angels and so many Muslims and Hindus seeing Jesus, we told the Lord in a joking way, "It sure would be nice if we could see an angel." Recently, Sharmila and I had the privilege of seeing the angel my daughter saw in our house. In the same spot where we saw the angel, my daughter had gold dust appear all over her head months earlier.

This is an exciting time to be living and serving Christ. Those who choose to be hungry, passionate, humble, and pliable will experience Jesus as He shows Himself in greater ways to reap the end time-harvest of souls. As we decrease and He increases, we will experience heaven on earth in our midst. We cannot work it up or earn it. It is simply a gift of grace. James 4:6 tells us that grace is given to the humble, "But he gives us more grace." That is why Scripture says: "God opposes the proud but gives grace to the humble."[13] The more we understand humility- that it is not about us or our accomplishments, but it's all about Jesus and how big He can be in our lives- the more we will experience Jesus in our personal affairs and ministry.

Psalm 138:6 tells us, "Though the Lord is on high, he looks upon the lowly, but the proud he knows from afar."[14] Jesus is BIG! One way we draw near to the living Christ is through humility. Jesus truly is not impressed with arrogant believers. As Psalms 18:27 puts it, "You save the humble but bring low those whose eyes are haughty."[15] Our Lord is very impressed and draws near to those that exhibit His Christ-like quality of humility.

Notice what Jesus says in regard to experiencing Him. In Matthew 11:28-30, He says, "Come to Me, all you who are weary and burdened, and I will give you rest. Take my yoke upon you and learn

[13] NIV
[14] NIV
[15] NIV

from me, for I am gentle and humble in heart, and you will find rest for your souls. For my yoke is easy and my burden is light."[16]

Sharmila and I cried out to experience the living Christ in preparation for our campaign in Moradabad. We realized that we were at a standstill and just going through the motions in ministry. We desired a greater measure of His manifested presence in our lives and ministry. We wanted a fresh touch and an easy yoke, rest and success in life and in ministry.

Jesus wants us to learn from or to experience HIM. What will we experience or learn from Him? We will be infused with His life and nature: lowliness and humility. Humility is recognizing everyday that in and of ourselves we don't have IT, but He does. We can tap into His joy, peace, love, faith, life, and so much more, by placing our dependence on Him.

In John 15:5, Jesus says, "…apart from Me you can do nothing."[17] Do you really comprehend what He said here? If you do, this could be your launching pad for a fruitful life and ministry! That is why John the Baptist said, "He must increase, but I must decrease"[18] when he saw Jesus. The more our lives are centered on Jesus, the more we will experience the living Christ in our midst.

It is not about chasing or seeking a feeling, manifestation, or personal recognition. Our lives must be about chasing and seeking after HIM. Jesus said in Matthew 6:33, "But seek first His kingdom and His righteousness, and all these things will be given to you as well."[19] The feelings, manifestations, blessings, and honor will come when we decrease and allow the nature of Jesus Christ to come forth in us.

[16] NIV
[17] NIV
[18] John 3:30, RSV
[19] NIV

According to Proverbs 22:4, "Humility and the fear of the Lord bring wealth and honor and life."[20] The fear of the Lord is reverence for His presence, acknowledging Christ in everything we do. It will keep us from doing things we should not be doing. Is there humility, a reverence, hunger, and awe for His presence in your life?

Part of reverence is giving all the glory to Him. Many believers are seeking the glory for themselves. That is not reverence for His presence. That attitude will not produce a lasting move of God. It will, in the long run, have just the opposite effect and hinder it.

Just filling ourselves with God's word, but not putting it into action, can lead to pride and spiritual dryness that has no power to change the spiritual and natural atmosphere around us. It is one thing to know about Jesus and His word, but quite another to experience Him and His word. Many Christians know know of Him, but do not really know or experience Jesus personally for themselves.

1 Corinthians 8:1 tells us, "Knowledge puffs up, but love builds up."[21] In Christian circles, many have become content attending conferences and hearing God's word, but not acting on it! All that does is puff us up with knowledge without transforming us. We need to go from head knowledge of God's word to practical experience of it on a regular basis, all with a spirit of humility.

Begin hungering for Jesus' manifested presence. Then allow His word to stir and transform your life and those you come into contact with. The less the focus is on you and the more it is on Christ and His word, the greater your experience of Jesus and the bigger Jesus will become in all areas of your life.

---

[20] NIV
[21] NIV

Robert Devens
Turbocharged for Miracles

Born and raised in Kansas City, Missouri, I came to the Lord through a very personal encounter at 16. Prior to my conversion, I had never sought the Lord but presumed that my family and I were Christians. I was in my bedroom, about to go to bed, when a large presence came into the room. Though the door was closed, I knew someone or something entered.

Shortly after sensing the presence, I started seeing visions of Christ dying on the cross. Instantly, the revelation of sin entered into my heart, and for the first time I understood what sin is and how I had rebelled against the Lord. Before this experience, I saw sin as more of a cultural thing- what was acceptable and what was not acceptable before men.

At the same time the weight of the revelation of sin was bearing down upon my soul, about to crush me, the revelation of His love pounded against my needy, broken heart. I was awakened to the divine reality that I was made for love and that I am His desire. I wept on my bedroom floor, repenting. Though I was born again in His love, I lacked leaders to disciple me for the first several years of my Christian life.

Later I joined a Spirit-filled church and was mentored by a missions pastor and several people from the congregation. Though my conversation experience was powerful and instantly life-changing, I still lacked any understanding of God and the Kingdom, specifically healing and deliverance. Unbeknown to me, many devils resided within me, seeking to bind me to sinful ways of thinking, speaking, and acting.

One lady who was discipling me, named Susan, gave me a book entitled *The Holy Spirit and His Gifts*. As I read through the book, intense desire was awakening within me. I soon discovered that there was more to spiritual life, much more than what I was experiencing. After several days of reading, I could not wait to finish the book before I called Susan and requested that we pray right away to receive the Spirit and His gifts.

I can remember the evening vividly. Susan bought pizza for all of us to eat before we prayed, and I was so nervous and filled with anticipation that I couldn't swallow anything. When the time came to pray, I sat on the floor and the others sat all around with their hands on me. They all started praying in quiet voices, and some prayed in tongues as I prayed internally. I was so nervous that I would speak out something that was not from God and that I would make the whole thing up to please those who were around me. I clamped my lips shut and said within, "Lord, I want everything You can give me. I give myself to You, fill me…"

The moment I prayed an electric current jolted my body, and I started to shake. After one second of this powerful electrical jolt, something very strange and difficult to express happened. It was as if my spirit left my body and was in another place. I could hear someone speaking very fast in tongues, and I thought, "Who is that?" Oh, it was me!

Though I was in the Spirit somewhere where there were inexpressible feelings of peace, joy, and love, I could faintly feel my body. Yet the Spirit had control over my speech. Several moments passed, and then my spirit re-entered my body, and I came to myself. The peace, joy, and love I felt stayed with me for many hours, and I received the gifts of prophecy and tongues.

Several months passed, and I started to work on staff at the church, being mentored by my missions pastor. I became disillusioned, however. I went on many hospital calls with my pastors, comforting many who were chronically sick, preparing for surgery, or on their deathbeds. I was so confused at what always transpired. We went and prayed, but I don't remember anyone being healed by our prayers.

I was faced not only with my own powerlessness but with that of those who were mentoring me. Pastoral care replaced any vision for a miraculous breakthrough of power. I remember asking my pastors, "Why isn't anyone being healed?" Their faces would often be just as puzzled as mine. Subconsciously, I began to receive and believe many lies, such as, "It is our duty to pray for the sick because we are pastors and leaders, but none of them are truly going to be healed." During those years, I prayed for many people who were ill, but no significant breakthrough came.

Early on, I attended a prophetic training session taught by Chuck Pierce. At the end of the seminar, he prophesied the following over me: "You are going to have a healing ministry in many nations of the earth." Such a word excited me; healing the sick must be fun when it actually works, I thought. I carried this word within me for many years.

As a result, I went to many conferences on healing and deliverance. I heard many good things, but I didn't see any healing or deliverance! When we prayed for the sick, and they were not healed, and no one prayed again. I can see now that subconsciously we determined that the sick person, if not healed after one prayer, would not get healed if we prayed again. No one I knew boldly preached healing or demonstrated it. Without a demonstration of the reality of healing, I felt the teaching was close to worthless.

The Lord began speaking to me about serving Him in the nations, specifically in India. So I went to a church planting school led by Floyd McClung. Immediately after completing the school, I went to India and lived among the indigenous Christians in the northern states. I ate what the Indians ate, lived the way they lived, and suffered a lot during this time.

While in India, I faced one problem after another, usually related to my health and demonic oppression. Within the first six months, I had to go to seven hospitals, and doctors were unable to diagnose my condition or provide medicine that brought lasting relief. I battled through constant discouragement, depression, and spiritual exhaustion. I sought the Lord for my own health, which led me to the shocking realization that I had no real faith of my own. I was drowning in frustration. I quickly became "merciful" to those who were suffering with various illnesses, where previously I would have judged them for their lack of faith.

I cried out to God for months for understanding, revelation, and power, but I felt like I was in a spiritual vacuum, face to face with my powerlessness. I soon realized that the power to heal the body and deliver the soul from demonic torment is the greatest avenue the Lord has for transforming the human heart and bringing forth repentance.

I heard about Global Awakening from a friend, and I timed my trip back to the USA so I could attend one of the ministry's conferences, which happened to be not too far from my city, in Ankeny, Iowa. When I arrived at the conference, I was thoroughly disappointed that Randy Clark was not able to come because of a back injury! I had learned to not "worship" a man but to honor the anointing on their lives. So I thought, "Well, maybe God will meet me through someone on their team." Will Hart was leading the meetings, and the conference was like rain upon cracked, dry soil. I felt like what 'died' in me was coming back to life!

Towards the end of the conference, there was an impartation time during the afternoon session. As I waited in line, I could feel the presence of the Lord lightly coming upon me. It felt like heaviness on my chest, face, and hands, but I also felt light on the inside. My heart was crying out for the "goods" to reach the nation of India.

The moment Will laid his hands on me, the current of heaven, the lightning of His power, jolted my body, and I began to shake with great intensity. The catcher had a hard time with me because every ounce of my body was being blasted! I had bruises on the back of my arms from where they tried to hold me and stop me from putting a hole in the floor! As I lay on the floor with the electricity flowing within me, the Lord began showing me visions and speaking deep within my spirit man about how He longed for the nations. His compassion for the nations began welling up within me. I began to weep and wail as my heart began to feel what He felt. I don't know how much time passed, but I was consumed with the moment.

When I got off the floor, I had to do something. I couldn't wait! I grabbed my friend's hand and said, "Let's go!" He looked at me a little strangely and said, "Where?" "We need to find sick people!" I replied intensely. We ran outside, and I began looking for anyone who had hearing aids, a cane, or a wheelchair.

We walked for about half a mile before we came upon a little park, with trees, benches, and a fountain in the middle with steps leading down to it. I saw in the distance a lady in a motorized wheelchair, and said to myself, "Hallelujah!" I made a beeline for her and, with a big smile, introduced myself. She was friendly, and I found out that she had degenerative disk disease and five of the disks in her lower back had been eaten away. She had terrible pain when she tried to get up and walk. I asked if I could pray, and she said, "Yes." Before I prayed, I asked if she was currently in pain. She replied that she was, and she would definitely know if God healed her.

I had her lean forward, and I placed my hand on her lower back and welcomed the Holy Spirit. I commanded pain to leave and miracle power to enter into her back. I asked her, "How are you now?" She replied, "Well, I don't know." I told her, "Do something that you could not do before." She grabbed both sides of armrests on her wheelchair and tried to get up. As she got 80 percent of the way up, her jaw dropped in shock, and she stood completely straight. She began to walk, slowly at first, but then picking up some speed. I immediately cried out, "Run!" She started running! She ran down the stairs to the fountain area and back up the stairs towards me! She came at me with speed and without stopping ran into me and gave me a big hug, which almost sent me to the ground!

I will never forget her smile, which was beaming with joy when she declared that there was absolutely no pain! I told her that God loved her and said some other things along those lines, but because I was so taken by the moment I forgot to lead her to the Lord! She left with some of her family, rejoicing in her complete healing.

The problem with seeing one miracle is that it makes us yearn for more. More Lord! Such desire was burning within me for more. When I was in the Global Awakening Conference, I heard about Bill Johnson and Bethel Church. I quickly made plans to go to the next conference, which was a healing conference! I was so amazed as many of their leaders shared testimonies of what God was doing. It stirred up such an appetite for the impossible. I thought to myself, "Now this church has the healing thing down! They are actually doing it!"

During a prayer time, I was focusing my attention on the Lord and crying out to Him for more power to reach the nations for His glory. Suddenly, I felt a huge invisible presence come before me. As the presence got closer, the heavier it felt upon my body. When it came really close, heavenly electricity zapped into my body and I shook so hard that I immediately hit the floor and scattered all the chairs near where I was previously seated.

I shook for about five to ten seconds violently on the floor, and suddenly the current stopped. As I looked up, I saw an angel standing in front of me. His face was difficult to make out because it was shining brightly. He had two wings that were smaller than I expected them to be, and he was about my height. He had on a short-sleeved baggy top that connected to what looked liked a short dress. It may have been all one piece but it was difficult to make out exactly because of the brightness of his face. One thing I really remember is that he had no hair on his arms.

Whatever he wanted to speak to me was projected from his mind and into my mind. While this was happening, everyone else in the room was just standing and praying, and they did not see what I could see. Evidently, this was an open vision given to only me. The angel's thoughts entered and spoke into my mind, "I am a miracle angel whom the Lord has sent to minister alongside you. You will not always see me, but know that I am with you, in your midst." Immediately after speaking this to me, he disappeared quicker than I could blink my eyes. I was rather stunned at the presence of this angel because his presence felt very similar to that of the Lord's. Probably because he was in His presence, I assume.

The last impartation from the Lord that equipped me for service in India took place in Tucson, Arizona, at Global Awakening's second school for healing. This time I was able to learn from Randy Clark, for he was the main speaker. During the entire conference I cried out in my inner man, saying, "God, if You don't anoint me and empower me, the sick in India will never know Your love, and many will never come to faith in You. For their sake and for the sake of Your glory, anoint me. I am not looking to a man, but You are the One who anoints men, and I look to You on Randy. I look to You, Holy Spirit." In between sessions I would sneak away, lay face down and with tears, cry out to God. I knew He heard me and was going to answer me.

When it came time for Randy to preach on impartation, I was yearning too deep for words. There are three levels of yearning I have experienced. There is yearning from the flesh, which is more or less making oneself choose to desire what God has for us. Second, there are the yearnings of the soul that deeply touch our emotions and consume our minds. But the yearnings of the spirit man are violent. They cannot be "stirred up" by any human effort. These yearnings literally frighten the soul in their intensity. The cry of the spirit man is so deep that it is beyond words. It almost seems foreign to the soulish realm.

As Randy shared story after story of how people were impacted by the ministry of impartation, my heart only pounded harder. Before the actual impartation prayer time, Randy explained that only those who felt electricity on their heads, shoulders, and/or hands should come near the stage first. As he began inviting the Holy Spirit, I started feeling trembling in my hands and on the top of my head. It was not violent shaking, but strong and gentle at the same time.

As Randy called those specific people forward, I started stepping forward and found it quite difficult to walk because the shaking was reaching my legs. As moments passed, the shaking increased. When Randy came down from the platform to lay hands on people, he started to first come in my direction and to stretch out his hand towards me. He was about 10 feet away from me when a bolt of electricity hit me and sent me crashing to the floor. I must have fallen back several feet; the electricity was hitting every area of my body, especially my hands. My hands were shaking so hard that they began to hurt. All of my muscles were in a constant spasm. My body was bouncing lightly on the floor, and my feet were shaking so hard that out of the corner of my eye, I saw my shoe, which was tied on tightly, come flying off. It felt like electricity, heat, and fire.

My body was sweating, and my shirt was soaked. I could hear the voice of the Lord speaking deep within my heart as I lay on the floor. "It is not by your strength or the determination of your soul that I will use you to heal nations. It is the purpose of My heart to show forth My healing love. It is because of My grace." He spoke more to me about my striving and attempts to "earn" His power through diligence in prayer, fasting, and disciplines.

As the electricity increased, my body was shaking so hard that my hands were literally a blur before my eyes. It seemed difficult to get enough oxygen because of the spasms. It wasn't like I was suffocating, but like my body was trying to get more air. As the shaking increased, I began thinking, "If this gets more intense, my body is going to be beyond repair! My body can't take more of this!" I found myself yelling out, "No more, Lord! No more! I can't take it anymore!" It is one thing to experience the peace of God, but another to experience the fire of His powerful presence. I was thinking, "Am I asking God to stop even though I have been crying out for more these past several years?!"

The intensity of the electricity began to decrease, and the shaking became limited primarily to my hands. Randy Clark started to prophesy over me, saying something of this nature: "I see you conducting healing meetings in the nations. I see you before thousands, and the Lord is going to heal multitudes through you. I also see you ministering to Muslim fanatics, Al Qaida members, and God is giving you grace now for those coming days. I see martyrdom happening around you, but I don't believe it will come to you…" His words echoed deep within my soul, because I have known for years that I would, one day, be ministering to the Muslim nations.

Several minutes went by, and the Global Awakening team came near to lay hands on me, which only increased the intensity of what I was feeling. As time passed, I went through moments of weeping as the Lord revealed His heart for the nations, and even moments of deep laughter. I was on the ground for about 50 minutes or so. Little did I know what kind of impact would soon come from this electric shock. This encounter was so outside of the box, beyond anything I had ever experienced. The intensity was the thing that overwhelmed me. God is big, and He is strong, and He can do anything!

I soon traveled back to India with great expectation. During my travels I was listening to many teachings from Todd Bentley. He stirred up new ideas about how to practically apply miracle power. One of Todd's approaches is to gather a crowd and boldly say, "Listen to me! Listen to me! The blind are going to see, the deaf are going to hear, and the crippled are going to walk! If not, I am a false prophet, and you can stone me!" I thought, "Wow, that is radical!" I took that model but dropped off the last part about being a false prophet and the stoning deal.

I started holding training sessions in Northern India, in areas where there is little or no Christian influence. My training was focused upon the Holy Spirit, impartation, spiritual warfare, and healing. I began to witness a total change in the atmosphere due to the presence of the Holy Spirit, with power and greater operation of the gifts of the Spirit. My training sessions became more fun with the power of the Holy Spirit present.

About 350 church planters, pastors, and house church leaders came to one three-day meeting, eager for the things of the Spirit. I prepared the people for impartation and the baptism of the Spirit. I told them that it would take time for me to come and pray for each person individually, and that it was not necessary for me to lay hands on them in order for them to receive what God desired for them, though He often uses yielded vessels.

As I went down the line praying, the power of the Spirit was present, and before I could even lay hands on many people, the Spirit of God would zap them good! People began to instantly speak in tongues, see visions, be delivered from demons, be jolted to the floor, and shake under the power of the Spirit. Afterwards, one man testified that while he was waiting for me to come and pray for him, he thought it would take too long, so he set his focus upon Jesus and remembered what I said. Suddenly, he saw Jesus walking through the midst of the people in the meeting! It was an open vision, and Jesus came directly up to him, laid His hand on him, and the power of God came upon him! Lives were so changed and impacted in just minutes! It was so wonderful to know in my inner man that I truly did receive grace, and that I could give it away.

In Unnao, Uttar Pradesh, India, I held a two-day healing meeting. It is difficult to hold healing meetings in Northern India for many days because Hindu radicals will gather to persecute and influence the police with false accusations of forced conversions to shut down the meetings. Many Hindus came to the meeting, and I called up all the deaf to demonstrate the power of God prior to preaching. About 10 people lined up front, and I had my team verify that they were deaf, either partially or completely. I quickly went down the line, sticking my fingers in their ears and commanding the deaf spirits to leave them. One by one people began to hear, almost instantly. Out of the ten, seven of them were instantly healed, including one seven-year-old girl who had been born deaf. Both of her ears opened instantly. After demonstrating God's compassionate love in power, the people, who were mostly villagers, were very attentive to hear of this God whose love they were seeing!

As I prayed a mass healing prayer, immediately the power of God began to flood the small hall in which we gathered. One lady who had suffered a stroke and was completely paralyzed on one side of her body, who could not properly care for herself or anyone else, was completely healed. She came forward and demonstrated her healing. You could see that the right side of her body was slightly atrophied from years of no use, but she regained complete control of her right arm and leg, and the right side of her face didn't droop anymore! While she was testifying, another elderly lady who had been completely blind in her left eye for eight years came forward. Her eye instantly popped open! I had her close her good eye, count my fingers and grab my finger, which she did with ease. The crowds went wild as the power of God shouted that Jesus is alive! One after another, people testified to the healing power of God. Some who had been afflicted with pain as long as 30 years were instantly set free.

The next day many more people came to the meeting, especially unbelievers. The word quickly spread from village to village about the sick being healed, especially the deaf people who were now hearing. At the next meeting, people began storming the front in hope of receiving a miracle. One lady brought her nephew to the meeting. He was 22 years old and was born completely deaf and mute. He'd never heard or spoken once in his life. His aunt grabbed his hand and pushed and pressed up to the front where I was ministering. My team was praying for many people and was trying to keep the masses off me so that I could properly minister. She pushed through my team and brought the young man up to me. I had my friend prepared to record miracles, and he started recording the moment I prayed. I put my fingers into his deaf ears and commanded, "In Jesus' name, I command this generational curse of deafness, be broken! Deaf spirit, I bind you and I command you to leave this man now! Get out!" I pulled my fingers out, and instantly he started to hear! Immediately I called out in Hindi, "Who brought him here? Where is his mother?" The lady came forward and identified herself as his aunt. She testified in front of everyone that he was indeed born deaf and mute. By snapping my fingers with his eyes closed, he demonstrated that he could hear out of both ears. I then prayed for his tongue, commanded it to be loosed, and the mute spirit to leave him. I looked at him and made the sound, "Mama, papa..." He clearly repeated me. I started to count in Hindi, and he repeated everything absolutely clearly. Everyone went crazy, astonished at what God was doing!

A young woman came up to me and told me that she had been tormented by demons day and night for seven years. I had her look steadfastly into my eyes, and I told her, "I am not speaking to you but to the tormenting spirits inside you. I am going to cast them out in Jesus' name." I looked into her eyes and commanded, "You tormenting demons! I command you, come out of her now!" Immediately she closed her eyes, her face contorted and, grabbing her head and hair with both hands, she fell to the ground. She started shaking as I gave a few more commands to those devils. Right away, the spirits left her, and the peace of God came upon her. She was instantly set free! It was fun and easy, I thought.

I did not understand how big these miracles were. These people were from villages in the surrounding areas, and Indian people live in extremely close community, whether they like it or not. Houses are small and usually made of mud, often with no doors. Since they live in such close proximity to each other, everyone knows everything about everyone else. Everyone in that village and surrounding villages knew about the young man who was born deaf and mute or the lady who had been demonized for years. In India, people view the afflicted, blind, crippled, maimed, and deaf as "cursed" by the gods, as the consequence of the family's sin or the sin of that person in a previous life. There is a stigma and cultural shame that plagues such families. When such heavenly love and power comes upon the afflicted, *everyone* quickly learns that the deaf and mute now hear and speak, the demonized are set free, and the blind see! Such miracles spread like wildfire, and the news that Jesus is healing the sick cannot be contained.

I was holding a three-day healing meeting during the evenings, where we minister the power of God and preach deliverance from sin through faith in Christ Jesus. But during the day we had some free time, and a believer called us over for lunch and to pray for a family member who was partially paralyzed.

On the way to the house, we were traveling in an old, rinky-dink van. I was sitting in the back seat gazing out the window. The scenery in India is never boring: rickshaws racing, women carrying heavy baskets on their heads, and cows eating trash always grab the eye. As we were crossing the intersection on the highway, my eyes landed on two men in their mid-twenties who were sitting on the highway divider, which was about three feet high and had grass and a few trees on top. One man made a hand sign to the other, and the moment I saw it, I immediately jumped up in my seat and shouted in Hindi, "Ruko, ruko, RUKO!"—stop! The driver hit the brake and swung over by the roadside as I looked at my friend. I said, "I think one of those guys might be deaf!"

I jumped out of the van and immediately crossed the street. The two men stared at me as I approached them with puzzled eyes. Upon reaching them, I tried to make conversation but they kept making signs that they could not hear nor speak, and kept shaking their heads, "No." I immediately said within my heart, "Hallelujah!" I was not saying this because they were deaf and mute, but because the God of all glory, the Lord God Almighty was about to break into time and forever change their history!

I put my hands together and made a sign that I wanted to pray for them. It is against the culture in India to say, "No," to a request because it is a face-keeping, people-pleasing way of life. The first deaf mute man nodded his head hesitantly. I placed my fingers into his ears and started to pray. He was a Hindu and did not understand how to "assume" the prayer position! He stared into my eyes, wondering what I was doing. I prayed with authority, "In the name of Jesus, I break this generational curse of deafness, and I command you deaf spirit, come out of him!" Instantly both of his ears popped open, and his eyes turned into saucers!

No wonder they were sitting on the highway divider. They were completely deaf, and the constant noise didn't affect them! I started snapping my fingers near his ears, and he could hear clearly. Without making another hand signal for prayer, I immediately cupped my hands around his mouth and prayed, "You mute spirit, I command you in Jesus' name, loosen this tongue that you have bound and leave! Generational curse of muteness break and tongue speak!" I leaned towards him and started to make simple sounds. He was instantly able to repeat what I was speaking!

With great joy I immediately turned to the healed man's friend who was also a deaf mute from birth and, without any hesitation, I placed my fingers in his ears and repeated the prayer. At first nothing happened at all, then I prayed twice more; The third time his ears opened, and he also began speaking!

What do you think was going through those men's minds? They were enjoying the shade on the divider as they suddenly saw a red van slam on the brakes and a white guy jump out and approach them! Did they have any faith? Absolutely not. Because they were Hindus and deaf. If they couldn't hear, how could faith come? It wasn't because of faith, but because of the goodness of God and His great desire to "save that which is lost" that these men heard. Without any understanding of what was happening when I was sticking my fingers in their ears, instantly they began to hear. In India, the car horn is used for everything, and on a highway divider their senses must have been overstimulated!

Though they both began to instantly hear and speak, we were not able to convey to them that Jesus Christ healed them; they had no concept of Him since they were born and raised Hindus. While trying to communicate with them, my friend came to understand that they could read and write. Both of these men were from a higher class of society and were privileged to go to a special school where deaf mutes could learn to read and write. We told them to come to the evening healing meeting to testify and to receive a Bible, the book about the God who healed them. They wrote down that they themselves were going to come, and they would bring all of their deaf-mute friends! Immediately these two men became our new evangelists! With hearts celebrating God's goodness, we departed.

With great joy, I anticipated the evening healing event. My time prior to the meeting was not spent "storming the heavens" in relentless intercession, which I had found to be fruitless in years past, but with thanksgiving for His presence that was upon me and for His word that cannot return void. When I arrived at the meeting, I met the two men. When it came time for me to speak, I shared the miracle story on the highway, which caused the crowds to shout for joy and look to God in great expectation. Both men came on stage, and I demonstrated that they could hear, and I gave each of them a Bible.

After the message, my team began to pray for various sick people, but I focused my attention only upon the deaf, mute, and blind. That night about eight deaf mutes came to be healed, and seven of them were instantly set free. It was so much fun, and it was so easy! They stood in line with great expectation, waiting for their chance to receive prayer. One by one they started hearing and then speaking. With every healing, more expectation grew in their hearts! One young man in his twenties, upon receiving prayer, instantly spoke with such clarity that I, without prior knowledge of his condition, would not have believed he was deaf and mute from birth! As I tried to sleep that night in the hotel room, I could only think about the amazing things Jesus did and how He demonstrated His love and kingdom with surpassing power.

I held a healing meeting in another city several hours drive away. Farmers came from surrounding villages to the meeting in search of mercy. I have noticed that if I focus upon healing the bodies of the sick, then salvations will abound. But if I focus all of my attention on preaching the word with a goal of repentance, very little fruit will come.

While I was preaching the mercy of God, I could see angels in the crowd! They were even in size, about 10 to 12 feet tall. Their bodies were somewhat transparent and glowing with heavenly light. There were four of them; two of them were hovering above the crowd, and two were standing on the ground. What I saw, I began to declare, knowing that my words of agreement would cause heaven to invade our little earth.

When it came time to pray for the sick, I called everyone forward, near the stage. I told them repeatedly that I didn't have to lay hands on them for God to work, and that His Spirit would sovereignly move upon them. I had them put one hand on the area of their body that was afflicted and lift the other hand up towards heaven. If they had multiple problems, they just put their hand on their heads.

I began to pray, inviting the presence of the Spirit, commanding the Kingdom of God to manifest in power, and, most of all, rebuking and commanding the devils of affliction and disease to leave their bodies. As I continued to release the Kingdom in power and rebuke the works of the enemy, I noticed out of the corner of my eye that a man who was wearing an all-white kurta (traditional male clothing, similar to a dress with sleeves worn over thin pants) was laying unconscious on the dirt-covered ground. I did not focus more attention upon him at that time because I was so wound up in prayer.

After a short prayer, we told the crowd to check their bodies and see if they were healed. Those who were healed were asked to come to the stage. After several people testified to their healings, the man in the white kurta came up to share. My friend and co-laborer, who was directing the testimonies, asked the man, "What happened to you!? Your entire back, legs, arms and head are covered in dirt!" The man explained that as we prayed, he felt the power of God shoot into his body like electricity, starting from the top of his head and going to the soles of his feet. Overwhelmed by the power of God, he fell over completely unconscious. When he came to himself, he immediately noticed that all of his pain and symptoms were gone! He had four chronic conditions and had pain throughout his entire body when he came to the meeting, but all of it was completely healed in a quick zap!

While he was sharing this from the microphone, I started thanking God in my heart! That miracle angel the Lord had sent my way was there, and he was going around blasting people with miracle healing power! What the man described as healing electricity was so similar to what I felt when I first encountered that miracle angel! It is so comforting to know that I am not alone, and that His hosts are taking ground with me!

In my memory I picture the crowds of people, like lost sheep, helpless and hopeless without a loving Shepherd. As I live more and more in the Spirit, this is my view of people. Prior to these life-changing encounters with God, I viewed Him as angry and people as condemned. The only important issue was repentance. Now the important issue is mercy. He who shows the most mercy at the end of the day wins!

It was during these several months of ministry and outreach that I first began to see most of the miracles happening among the deaf. In less than one year, I personally prayed for and witnessed more than 100 deaf people healed. Of those, 25 had been born deaf. But as the months continued, my hunger burned for those who were blind.

After the fresh baptisms of power, I had no idea that I was going to see so many miracles come forth in so little time. I was in India on a very low budget, unable to hold any "big" meetings. But even small meetings proved to be extremely fruitful and fun! One such meeting was in a primitive village area. Only 350 people came to the rented hall. To be honest, I was very discouraged by the numbers. As the miracles grew, I wanted the ability to orchestrate big events with lots of people, but this was not possible in most areas where I ministered, because of persecution and radical opposition.

When I stood in that small hall looking at the people, I challenged them and said, "How many of you have a friend, family member, neighbor, or enemy who is deaf, mute, or blind? Raise your hand if you know someone." Slowly people started to raise their hands around the room, and with repetition, more people responded. I then stated, "Bring those people to this meeting tomorrow, and they will be healed!" I ministered that evening, focusing more on the Word with eager expectation for the following night.

As I returned the following evening, that small hall was about to burst with people. They were like sardines! You had to step over bodies to get to the front. Before I preached, I boldly proclaimed that God would do mighty works in our midst. I called up all the deaf, mute, and blind to the front and lined them up before the crowd that numbered about 600 people. I had my team confirm that they were truly afflicted.

Using our normal routine, I had a prayer volunteer with every deaf, mute, or blind person. The volunteers' main responsibility was to agree with me in prayer and immediately test the person's hearing, speaking, or sight. While I quickly went from person to person praying, I always started with the deaf people first, because I had an 80-90 percent success rate ministering to them. As I prayed, my fellow pastor would pray for all the sick from the microphone. This helped to keep the crowd's mind upon the Lord instead of just gawking as we prayed, or becoming restless. As people began receiving their miracles, the pastor would stop praying and transition into having people who were healed give testimonies, one by one. If the "flow" went well, we would have testimonies lined up, which gave us more time to pray. I found this structure worked very well, especially in ministry among villagers, semi-illiterate, or illiterate people.

I first prayed for a man who was born deaf and mute, and instantly his ears popped open! One after another deaf ears just popped open with little prayer. After the deaf, I quickly started praying for the mute. One young boy, 13 years of age, had never spoken an intelligible word in his life. While praying for him, I commanded the mute spirit to loosen his tongue and commanded him to be healed and speak. Immediately he started counting in Hindi after me and I had him say, "Jesus just healed me." We called up his relative who confirmed that the boy was indeed born mute.

Another lady in her late 40's (who looked closer to 70!) instantly started hearing and speaking after we broke the generational curse of deafness and muteness. Her daughter was present, and we had her confirm her mother's condition. We asked her, "Who healed your mother?" She did not know what to reply, and after several moments of silence, she pointed her finger at me. I quickly took the opportunity to instruct her and teach the crowd that no one can do such amazing and marvelous works. It is only in the name of Jesus Christ and in His name alone that people are healed!

After every testimony, we always ask the people who healed them and teach them that it was Jesus Christ. On more than one occasion, Hindus seeking healing came from many hours away only to prostrate at my feet, begging for healing favor. This kind of act puts such distaste in my mouth. As I ventured into this miracle calling, I have a greater revelation after each miracle that I am nothing but dust and completely helpless and hopeless without His goodness. There is a saying in Hindi- "*Guru devataon se barkar hai,*" which means, "The spiritual teacher is greater than the gods." Indians give more honor to their teachers than to the gods they worship, because the teacher is the mediator of their relationship with the god. Therefore, there is much worship of men in their society.

After all the mutes began to speak, the blind too began to see! Though their sight was not always completely restored to 20/20, they were able to count my fingers from afar, which they could not do before.

That night only one lady who was partially deaf was not healed. The majority received a full healing, and the remaining few received partial healings. After the miracles, we boldly preached repentance and faith in Christ as the only savior from sins.

I have found it very easy to see Hindus and Muslims come to faith in Christ, especially when their blind son starts to see or their deaf mother begins to hear, or their crippled daughter begins to walk! Again, it is our powerlessness that produces difficulty in evangelism.

What do I usually feel when I pray for people? Sometimes nothing, but more often I have various sensations. When I prayed for the lady in the wheelchair in the park in the U.S., I felt absolutely nothing, and neither did she, but she was completely healed. Usually, though, I feel trembling in my hands or in my legs. I can sometimes feel electricity shoot from my arms through my hands. At other times, I feel a "weight" of authority on me. It feels like a presence over my head, neck, and upper body, and I know that what I am speaking has power behind it.

One of the most interesting things about the manifestation of power I feel in my body is that it does not always result in a healing. At times I feel the trembling, heat, and electricity, and often the person receiving feels the same, but they are not always instantly healed. Since I travel from place to place, I don't have the privilege to follow up with all the people to know if their healings manifested later. But many times a miracle does happen instantaneously when I feel these manifestations.

For example, one evening at a healing event, I called up all the deaf, as I usually do. As I went down the line, deaf person after deaf person was instantly healed. I came to one lady who was completely deaf in her left ear. I commanded the curse of deafness to break, as I did previously with all the others who were now hearing, but nothing happened. I skipped her and went on. Afterwards I made my way back and prayed again, commanding that deaf spirit to leave, and then I released the Kingdom into her ear. Again, nothing happened. I prayed all sorts of prayers I knew worked in the past but this time to no avail.

While I was frustrated and my finger was in her ear, I started to pray, "God, I tried everything I know! I rebuked this and bound that, and nothing is happening! If You don't send Your power, nothing is going to happen!" No sooner had those words came out of my mouth than my right shoulder, arm and hand started trembling greatly, and I felt an electric wave of energy shoot out of my arm through my finger into her ear. I pulled my finger out of her ear, and the moment I tested her hearing, she smiled and stated she could hear just fine!

All of these miracles took place within months of receiving the heavenly power through the ministry of impartation.

Don Foster
Ministering in Power in Mozambique

"Missionaries always get the greatest revelations of Jesus," I concluded after a missionary came to speak in my church in the 1980's. Ever since then, I have wanted to be a missionary. My spirit heard the invitation and wanted to scream, "Here I am, send me!"

But, in my congregation, it seemed that only the anointed, holy or beautiful people could minister, or those who were friends of the pastor or, more importantly, members of his family. The only way open was to serve under a leader and then be raised up, but all the leadership positions were filled. Thus, ministry opportunities would only open when the one you were serving under was raised up, died, or left the church.

I wanted to be worthy and anointed enough to serve the Lord as a missionary, but I never had "the stuff." "Little ole me" was never equipped, empowered, or commissioned to go.

Then Randy came to our church. He preached that God can use "little ole me." I got excited and gnawed on that message like a little puppy with a great big bone. When Randy left, the big bone was still there, but things continued as they were. What was I supposed to do with that message, with nowhere to minister? I knew I was called, but I didn't know where to go.

When I looked ahead at the church's schedule of upcoming speakers, I did not see Randy Clark, Bill Johnson, or Heidi Baker listed. They were doing their thing and going into all the world. I wanted God to use "little ole me" like that. So, I flew across the country to see Randy speaking in Toronto in May 2005 for a week of Soaking School at the Toronto Airport Christian Fellowship (TACF). THAT changed everything.

I found out what I should have already known. I could experience God's presence outside my church! I could actually be used by God without being inside the four walls of the church or in a position of "leadership." I did NOT have to wash toilets or serve for countless years in Sunday school and yard sales to get anointed enough to pray for the sick. Hallelujah!

All the politics, drama, and hierarchy in my local church now seemed like a tempest in a teapot as I soaked in God's presence so far away. God seemed so big, yet accessible, there on that soaking carpet. I tasted freedom, and I wanted MORE! I was drunk on the anointing and presence of God.

I went back to TACF for another drink in August 2005. John Arnott taught that the anointing is transferable, and I realized no one in church had to die for me to get it. Randy preached about impartation. I went up front to get some as fast as I could.

"This is what I have always wanted," I thought.

When Randy prayed for me, I was slain in the Spirit and lay on the floor with a new revelation: I have wasted so many years striving for this anointing that's been here for me on this carpet floor all these years.

As I lay there, literally stuck to the floor, I was thinking, "What now?"

The Lord whispered, "China."

As soon as I could get up, I staggered to Randy's Global Awakening table and signed up for the upcoming trip to mainland China. Two months later, I was there. Our team witnessed an amazing move of God. In meeting after meeting, there were waves of God's presence: one of repentance, another of deliverance, then joy, and finally, rolling-on-the-floor laughter. It looked just like Toronto- only Chinese-ier.

The last meeting was held in a small country church. I prayed for a little old Chinese lady who had not stood or walked in eight years. She did both that night all by herself, in Jesus' name. The whole church celebrated this miracle with her.

Many people were healed in those meetings. Demons were cast out. Some women on our team of ten commanded a demon to come out of a young possessed woman. When the demon came out, the women spoke for the first time in 10 years! The next day, she clothed herself, fed herself, and sang in church. It was so exciting.

That trip was a major turning point in my walk with the Lord and my ministry. I got it that God could use all the "little ole me's," like those of us on this trip. But, I needed more. I had seen so much fruit in such a short time, but I needed more instruction and more anointing. I went to Randy's Healing Fusion School 2 in Pennsylvania and other meetings, wherever I could find them. I just wanted to see more healings, more often.

Next, I fulfilled a dream and a vow to go to Mongolia. I didn't go with Global Awakening, but I preached a page right out of Randy's missions manual about "How to Receive a Word of Knowledge." As a result, we saw many people healed.

In Mongolia, a very timid man who had hardly ever been to church, much less spoken up or prayed for someone, gave a word of knowledge. In response to that, a man came forward who had not had any feeling in his foot for years due to frostbite. We saw God heal him! The man that was healed was so happy. The man who prayed was so encouraged in his faith. I was even more hungry to be used by God.

Flying to the healing schools and conferences where Randy was speaking really built me up in the Holy Spirit. Randy often preached on impartation, and I would always be first in line to receive.

On the flight back home from the first conference in Toronto, I wondered, "Did I get anything?"

Then as I was leaving the long-term parking at the airport, I led the guy in the tollbooth to the Lord. That's when I realized, "I got something!"

I joined the hospital visitation ministry of my church so I could practice praying for the sick. They sent me to pray for a little girl in a coma. The girl's father had been drinking and passed out while floating on a raft in a pool. While he slept, his daughter fell into the pool and drowned. When he awoke and found her lifeless on the bottom, he had no idea how long she had been there.

The father and paramedics used CPR to get her breathing, and the hospital placed her on a machine that breathed for her, but the doctors said she would die. They said, if somehow she lived, she would be permanently brain damaged and live out her life in a vegetative state because no brain waves had been detected. After I prayed a nice little I'm-here-from-the-church-to-comfort-the-family prayer, the nurse tried to remove the life support. As soon she disconnected the machine, our little patient stopped breathing and started to die.

The nurse reconnected the machinery to keep her alive.

I got out of the I-am-here-visiting-from-the-church mode and into praying-like-her-little-life-depends-upon-it mode. After this intense prayer, she opened her eyes. Her mother snapped out of her depression and threw off the weight of despair she'd been carrying to cling to this one ray of hope. She told everyone that her baby would live while the doctors and nurses maintained that the girl would die.

I called on my men's group at church, and we all prayed fervently. Tom Craig and Elijah Aakpana came to visit and pray. On the third day, the little girl rose again- just like Jesus. Praise God!

This resurrection and the following three days were nothing short of miraculous. She relearned how to sip from a straw, eat, talk, and finally to walk again. She was released directly from ICU to go home, without spending any time in rehab. Soon after, she celebrated her fourth birthday party in perfect health with no brain damage!

The family and friends who had previously given up hope praised God for the miracle and started going to church. The father went to AA instead of going to prison for felony child neglect, the charges he was facing if she had died.

My faith soared. I began to pray for the sick like I was taught in Healing School. People recovered! At first, it was only headaches, but I marveled.

I thought, "Wow! I am not even on the platform or in a 'position of ministry,' but I am ministering."

I was not yet truly free. It took years of following the Lord and serving in ministry before I could get out of my old church, and then years for my old church to get out of me. The process was costly and painful.

My freedom did not sit well with the leaders in my church. When I gave testimonies of healings and asked questions, they threw me out of the hospital visitation and homeless ministries. They told me I could not "minister" anymore, as if being in a position in that church was the only possible way to serve in Christ. I was free, but I had no place to go. I felt rejected and dejected.

To show me who is actually in charge, the Lord placed me in two ministries outside the church: hospital chaplaincy and homeless ministry. As a chaplain, it was my job to go from room to room praying for the sick. This was far better than going only when sent to one person on occasion.

In serving the homeless, we distributed 5,000 blankets, food, socks, and wool hats. I witnessed 100 times more fruit in these ministries than I ever saw through my church. The anointing breaks all bondages!

At TACF in 2007, Randy preached about prophecy. Afterwards, he prayed for practically everyone in the building. During this time of impartation, Randy said to me, "I see many foreign coins in your pocket. You are going to be a missionary." I was ecstatic. That was exactly what I wanted. I was anointed and commissioned by angelic visitations. The only remaining puzzle pieces were where to go and when.

In Randy's book, *There is More*, I learned more about impartation and ministry. In tears, I read about Heidi and Roland Baker's ministry in Mozambique, Africa. They were seeing people healed, the dead raised, and churches planted. They desperately needed more people to help. I decided, then and there, that I wanted to go to Africa and serve the Lord in Iris Ministries.

I signed up for the Iris Ministries Harvest Mission School (as it is now called) and prepared to go. Two days before I was scheduled to leave, my business sold, giving me the opportunity to stay in Mozambique and serve after the school ended.

Two years later, I am still living my dream of being a missionary here in Mozambique. We regularly see the deaf hear, the lame walk, and the blind see. Weekly, a small team of us Jesus Lovers go out to reach the poorest people we can find in little forgotten villages. We see so many people saved and healed, often, everyone we pray for is healed.

In our last outreach to Namaacha, a border town in Mozambique near Swaziland and South Africa, an old man who was blind since birth was healed. In May 2009, during our second mission trip to the neighboring country of Zimbabwe, we saw five blind or partially blind people healed in one day. So many people were coming forward for prayer on that trip that we had to line them up and pray for them in groups. Praise God! Zimbabwe is suffering in many ways due to the complete collapse of the economy. It is ripe for revival at this very moment and needs more missionaries to come now. Maybe this is your opportunity?

During our third mission trip to Zimbabwe in August 2009, everyone was healed in the last four services in a row (except for two cases). After that trip to Zimbabwe, I was so sick from exhaustion that I detoured to attend Randy's Healing School in Durban, South Africa. I was healed, so refreshed, and encouraged in that healing school.

The last time Randy prayed for me, I asked him to pray again for humility as he did once after he preached a message on the subject. I believe God gives grace to the humble, and that grace is required to be used in healings, signs, and wonders. Randy has this humility. And, I just want more; I am so greedy for God and His ministry to the saints and evangelism, that I changed my middle name to "More."

I am living my dream of being a missionary in Africa. I am the director of Project Benjamin with Iris Ministries in Boane, Mozambique. We act as a transition place for men who were raised in the care of Iris Ministry, but have not yet finished school. For example, in 2009 we were working with Helder in his third year of medical school, Pedro in his third year of engineering school, Admiro in his first year of law school, and Vasco in the 12th grade, who aspires to be a teacher. We are also working with two young men in 11th grade, one in 10th grade, one in 8th grade, and one in 6th grade. And Alfonso, who has become a truck driver. All know Jesus and are seeking more of Him.

Weekly, our little evangelism team does outreaches from Boane into local and remote villages in Southern Mozambique. We showed the Jesus film in Changaan and practically everyone accepted Jesus. We have seen so many people healed. Always, people come forward to be healed of stomachaches, backaches, headaches, and all sorts of sicknesses. Always, they go away better. Often everyone is healed. All praise and glory be to the One in whose name we pray.

Being a missionary is so very rewarding. It is an extreme honor to minister to some of the poorest people in the world through evangelism, discipleship, teaching, healing, bringing food and mosquito nets, building houses, paying for school fees and uniforms, preparing people to find jobs, and so much more. Life is never boring here, but we could use more help.

Even though I am living my dream of being a missionary in Africa with Iris Ministries, I still want more. I pray for the sick, and they recover in Jesus' name. Blind eyes open, but I have not yet raised anyone from the dead. I have met people who have been raised from the dead. I have met people in Iris Ministries, like Surprise Sithole, who have raised the dead. I want to do that. At first it was just headaches, why not raise people from the dead, too?

I heard Bill Johnson say in a CD teaching something like, "The fastest way to be launched into supernatural ministry is to go on a mission trip with Randy Clark." I would like to add that going to the Harvest Mission School of Iris Ministries in Pemba, Mozambique, is the fastest way to become a missionary.

There is so much more of God than most people ever experience in their local churches. God can use you in the mission field. Please come to the Iris Harvest Mission School and then join Iris Ministries in Africa. Or go into some other part of the world and preach the Gospel. Jesus is coming soon. Only the pure of heart will see His face, and only the obedient will live with Him.

George[22]
Brain Tumor Victim Turned Victor

How did I get here? I suddenly awoke to find myself lying in the back of an ambulance, with no idea how I had gotten there. I had an oxygen mask on, an IV, and paramedics were swarming around me. I could barely remember what had happened over the last day, a beautiful August day in 2003.

I had been enjoying the sunshine, and my wife was due to give birth to our first child any day now. But how did I end up in this ambulance? Then one of the paramedics said to me, "You've had a seizure." How could I have had a seizure? I was in perfect health, very physically fit, and never had a seizure before in my life.

"We're going to take you to the ER," he said. I couldn't argue. At the emergency room, after a CAT scan, the doctors told me I could go home but needed to make an appointment with a neurologist right away. A few days later, I saw a neurologist, who ordered an MRI of my head. Meanwhile, my wife went into labor, and while she was recovering from a C-section at one end of the hospital, I was at the other end getting an MRI.

[22] Pseudonym used to maintain anonymity for professional reasons.

The next two weeks were a whirlwind with the excitement and exhaustion that accompany having a newborn baby. We barely noticed the doctors' growing concern when they ordered additional tests for me. Then, at the end of August, when my daughter was just over two weeks old, we got the news- I had a brain tumor.

As a scientist with a Ph.D. and one who knows something about the brain, I sat in my car at the hospital reading the radiology report. I exploded in tears and grief, because I knew how untreatable these kinds of tumors are; essentially no one survives more than a few years, regardless of treatment. My worst nightmare had suddenly become reality.

In an instant I went from having a new family, a promising career, and a happy life, to facing a medical death sentence. The brain tumor was the latest event in a year that had already been difficult. Ever since we had started an intercessory prayer group at our mainline evangelical church a year earlier, our lives had been filled with medical emergencies- several trips to the emergency room, a miscarriage, and now the seizure and brain tumor. Even so, we had persevered in doing what we thought to be an important form of prayer ministry: praying against various principalities and cults in our city. Just a couple of weeks before the seizure, by chance we had run into a woman canvassing in a nearby park for a local outreach center for a large religious cult. I had spent some time interacting with the woman directly, and right afterward we went to work praying against the group's activities.

My wife didn't sleep well the night we learned of the brain tumor. While she sat up praying and nursing our newborn, she remembered a particularly vivid dream she had had several weeks before. In that dream, she saw an evil face and heard an evil voice that identified itself by an unusual, memorable name. The evil being said that it was going to kill us.

My wife told me later that at the time she had prayed a short prayer asking God's protection and then forgot about it. The dream had come to mind briefly a couple of additional times, but she didn't give it much weight and hadn't said anything about it to me. Now, as she remembered the dream, she felt that God was telling her she needed to know the name from the dream. She typed the name into Google, and, to her surprise, it turned out to be the name of the codebook used by the same cult that we had been praying aggressively to counter only a few weeks before.

That caught my wife's attention. She also remembered a time about a month before when she had—uncharacteristically—sensed that the Lord was speaking to her about a time in our future. She had written down her strong impression: that the Lord wanted us to know Him as we never had before, that some things must soon happen that we could not stop, but we could choose whether to greet them with fear or with faith—and our lives depended on the choice we would make. My wife had shared this word with me, and we had discussed it at the time, suspecting that if the Lord was going to give us such a strong word, we would likely need it, but we had no idea beyond that what the word might mean.

Early the morning after the medical diagnosis and these midnight musings, my wife came to wake me. When she told me the name she had heard in her dream and what she'd learned by Googling it, I was still in bed waking up. I suddenly became agitated, as if I had just drunk a gallon of coffee. I had the sense that we needed to pray right away. My wife prayed, addressing the name she had heard in her dream: "If there's a spirit named such-and-such, leave my husband alone in Jesus' name." No sooner had those words left her lips then I suddenly leaped out of bed and began violently thrashing around on the floor, screaming "Nooooo!"

I was fully conscious, so I was not having a seizure. In fact I even told my wife, "Don't call 911, I'm not having a seizure," to which she responded that that was clear enough, but something weird was happening. It was as if I had reflexes all through my body that were making my body do things, and my mouth say things, that I wasn't telling it to do. Emotionally I did not feel upset, but my body was reacting very strongly to something.

We knew almost nothing about deliverance, despite having spent four years as part of a church-planting team for a charismatic church they hadn't yet grown much in the exercise of spiritual gifts. Even so, my wife started commanding demons to leave me just in case. My head would whip around and scream "No!" at her every time she said the name from her dream, the religious group it was associated with, or the words "tumor" or "seizure."

I tried to say, "I belong to Jesus," but my throat would lock up when I got to the word "Jesus." I was perplexed at this point, because I had always thought that Christians can't be demonized. It was hard to argue that with myself though, since I knew I was a Christian (and, yes, even a "tongues-talking, spirit-filled" Christian). Yet, I also seemed to be violently manifesting demons.

We thought of trying to send the demons out somewhere, but we didn't have any pigs around. Maybe our cat? No, we didn't want a demonized housecat running around. We figured maybe we could send the demons into the squirrels outside or something. We didn't know what we were doing.

After about half an hour, the manifestations subsided, and I was tired and hoarse. It was clear to both of us that any demons present had not been successfully cast out, but had just decided to calm down for a while. In fact, I heard a voice in my head saying, "we're too powerful." My wife later told me that in witnessing this and many equally jarring demonstrations in the weeks that followed, she would have expected to have totally flipped out, but the Holy Spirit was so present to her that she remained inexplicably composed.

My wife immediately called the leadership of our mainline evangelical church and asked them to come over right away to help us. We first tried calling the missions pastor, since he was the most charismatically inclined, but he was gone, ministering somewhere in Latin America. Five pastors and senior leaders arrived within the hour, but they didn't know anything about deliverance ministry, nor did they believe in it. They just started praying, and I immediately started manifesting again. So they prayed some more and sang some songs, but all I did was manifest all the more. Singing songs about the blood of Jesus didn't seem to help. After a while, they decided it was time for them to leave. Later I saw one of them, a young seminarian, who said that he had helped by holding my feet down. I wasn't sure how to respond but I did thank him.

Also trying to be helpful, the senior pastor of our church—who had not been in the group that came over to pray for us—visited a few days later. We had looked forward to his visit, hoping for some help at last in getting free. Instead, genuinely meaning to help, he counseled us not to get our hopes up but to prepare to die well, lest we lose our "faith" when hoped-for healing did not come. He told us about a woman he knew who had held out in her struggle against a brain tumor longer than the doctors had expected, but who was, nevertheless, just then about to die.

We then started trying to find people who knew about deliverance but couldn't find any. For the next week, I was very depressed. What was the point of bothering going to work, doing science, and trying to figure out how the brain works, if mine was broken and I was going to die in a few years anyway? "Why me, God?" I was thinking. I began to pray and fast for days at a time, like I had never done before.

Medically, there wasn't anything of use to be done. Now, we're not anti-medical fanatics. Remember, I'm a scientist who happily works for the "establishment." Still, after reading all the scientific literature indicating that no treatment—whether chemotherapy, radiation, surgery, or all of them put together—could even prolong survival, and knowing that a biopsy was more dangerous than surgery, opted against any of these pointless interventions. (As I often ask those who cite that inane piece of misinformation that we only use 10 percent of our brains, which part of *your* brain would you like to have removed?). Instead, we were aggressively seeking help from the Lord.

I grew up in a conservative, evangelical church where no one ever talked about healings and miracles for today, or about deliverance ministry. One time someone in the church exercised the gift of speaking in tongues and, when they did so, they immediately also received the gift of a one-way trip to the church exit.

My wife also grew up in a mainline, evangelical church. So we had little framework for healing, but I began to think that if God still heals today, I'm going to find out, or else I'll die trying. I knew that Pentecostal and Charismatic people seemed to know something about healings and miracles, but they scared me. When I was in high school, I once went to a charismatic Episcopal church service. People started falling over and doing weird things like shaking and laughing. I left and never went back.

Then, in late 1994, I was spending a year abroad in the UK, when I heard about some people who had come from a revival in Toronto. One of my friends urged me to go to their services in the UK where I was living. I went (reluctantly), and I saw people falling over, laughing, crying, and shaking.

The people said that God had given them the Holy Spirit, and that it was transferable. I remember feeling both a sense of fear about what was happening and at the same time a sense that I didn't want to miss out if it really was God. I finally went forward for prayer, on guard and ready to bolt for the door at the first sign of heresy. Instead I found people praying gently for me to receive the Holy Spirit, more of God's love, and similar non-scandalous prayers. I felt nothing resembling the presence of God at the time—I just stood there with my hands and teeth clenched, while others fell to my right and my left. Eventually I left the meeting.

Within a few days, while I was praying alone one night, I suddenly felt the presence and love of God come on me like never before. I literally fell out of my chair and laughed and cried the whole night. For the first time, I had not only known, but also felt the love of God. I didn't know what was happening exactly, but I knew that God was showing me His love.

About five years later, I described the experience to a friend, and my friend said that I had received the Holy Spirit. "Is that what you call it?" I responded. My friend said that since I had received the Holy Spirit years earlier, I could probably also speak in tongues. Then what do you know, I found that I could speak in tongues!

As wonderful as all of that was, the people from Toronto came and left the UK barely a week later. In their wake was the Holy Spirit and a lot of controversy, but essentially no teaching. So I still had very little framework with which to understand the work of the Holy Spirit and healing as they related to my present brain tumor crisis.

In the days and weeks following the seizure, we talked to many of our friends, asking them to fast and pray for us. We also came to realize that taking on principalities over cities by ourselves in intercessory prayer was—technically—a bad idea. We came across John Paul Jackson's book *Needless Casualties of War* and felt even worse. So we got on our faces repenting, because we saw that we had not been going about spiritual warfare the right way.

On September 8, a closet charismatic from our church called and told us about a city-wide intercessory prayer group (under the C. Peter Wagner covering) that normally didn't pray for individuals, but he thought maybe they could help me if I went early before the meeting began. We immediately got in the car and were there within an hour. I couldn't legally drive because of the seizure, so my wife and newborn accompanied me on every such prayer outing.

I walked in, and the group's leaders said they had heard through their prayer network that I was demonized. They said they could take care of that, no problem. They told me to sit down and started asking me questions. Was I involved in the occult? Did I have Freemasons in my family, etc.? I said I wasn't into the occult, but what was wrong with having all those high-ranking Freemasons in my family?

They began to pray, and I began to manifest violently again. I smashed my glasses. They cast out all kinds of demons, and most of the time I retched and writhed and barfed uncontrollably as they cast them out. (Yes, the prayer ministers had bound the demons, so, no, they "shouldn't" have manifested in such unseemly ways, but the demons didn't seem to be following the rulebooks). This went on for an hour and a half, at which point the group had to start their regular meeting. I was still manifesting, however, and they felt bad leaving me manifesting demons during the prayer meeting. So, some of them took me to a side room and continued ministering. After about another hour and a half of screaming, barfing deliverance, I suddenly felt very peaceful, like the Lord's presence was all around me, and I started laughing. "Who is laughing?" the deliverance ministers demanded. Was it a demon? I answered no, that I was laughing because I felt so peaceful. They concluded that we were done for the evening.

I decided that I liked this group of people. Afterwards, the leader of the intercessory prayer group told me that a man named Pablo Bottari was coming to town the very next week and suggested that I should go see him to learn more about deliverance. I had never heard of him before, but I figured it would be a good idea to learn more about deliverance ministry.

So I called the woman who was organizing his visit. She had worked with Benny Hinn (I had heard of him before as the guy in the flashy white suit) and Kathryn Kuhlman (though I hadn't heard of her). And—coincidentally?—she said that she herself had been healed of a terminal brain tumor over thirty years ago in a Kuhlman miracle service.

This woman ran "healing rooms" and sounded very nice on the phone. She invited me to come that very night. I asked her what healing rooms were. "Is it some kind of New Age thing? I'm a Christian; I'm not into that New Age stuff." She assured me that they were Christians, so I went. Once I was satisfied (having given them quite an extensive doctrinal test) that they were actually believers, I let them pray for me.

The healing rooms' team started asking about my family, and then started breaking generational curses and things like that, at which point I manifested violently and vomited for nearly two hours. There was one deliverance minister and two others in the intercessory position. One dear lady was on one side, and she was earnestly saying "the blood of Jesus!" over and over again while someone else vigorously commanded the demons to leave. The next thing I knew, my head wrenched around, and I screamed at the poor woman.

The following week, we all went to hear Pablo Bottari for three nights of teaching. Suddenly, all that was happening to me started making sense. Not only did I understand my own predicament, but I began to reflect upon past experiences, trying ineffectively to minister as a lay church leader to people who, in retrospect, had been severely demonized. I cried as I thought about all the people who had come to me and my wife in previous years of ministry whom we had not known how to help. All we had known how to do was to take them to alcohol dry-out centers, try to persuade them not to commit suicide, and attempt to prevent other church members from freaking out when these individuals' voices changed mid-prayer to utter cackling threats of "revenge." If only we'd known years before.

Pablo was very nice and ministered to us personally. I realized that when my wife was pregnant and the baby was in a breech position, it had not been a good idea to burn mugwort on her little toes to try to get the baby to turn. We later learned that the herb, which we had purchased from a New-Agey natural foods store, had been dried in the sun to soak up its spiritual energies and that the related acupressure technique of moxibustion was designed to move *qi* around, thereby achieving harmony with universal life-force energy. We had only tried it because we'd read a medical journal article attesting to the technique's effectiveness in turning breech babies. At the time, we hadn't cared *how* the practice worked, only that scientists said it was *effective*.

Pablo said this amounted to invoking spirits. It didn't work for us, and it was yet another door in a long list of openings for the demonic that needed shutting. We also concluded that it had been a bad idea for my wife to visit a chiropractor who similarly promised to unblock the flow of energy and coax the breech baby to turn. All of us, including the healing rooms ministers, also realized that it was not a very good idea to keep yelling "the blood of Jesus" while casting the demons out, as it only riled them up without making them go anywhere. At the end of three days of teaching, Pablo invited those who wanted more power for deliverance ministry to come forward for impartation. I eagerly went forward.

Then in early October, about a week or two later, I was sitting in my office, thinking scientific thoughts, when all of a sudden the power of God fell right in my office. This was a new experience, or at least, it hadn't happened in my office before. I almost fell out of my chair. "Come out of the desert!" I heard, in a booming (but not audible) voice in my spirit. "What does that mean?" I wondered.

Then the Lord said, "How many days since the tumor?" I counted them up, and it had been 40 days since I found out about the tumor. I was wondering if that meant something. Then the Lord said not to worry about it, that He would heal the tumor, and that, in the meantime, I was to go out and pray for sick people, and He would work miracles through my hands. Well, that sounded really weird, but I figured it wasn't a good idea to question the Lord about this sort of thing, so I guessed that God would make it clear.

Two weeks later, I flew out to visit my family in another state, and they were going to have some friends pray for me. Some of the people who wanted to pray for me, it turned out, also practiced Reiki, so I politely refused their offer and high-tailed it out of there. After having already gone to so much trouble to get rid of demons, I didn't feel inclined to invite any more in!

By this point, I had learned that having Freemasons all through the family was a problem. So I got my family to pray through the long, long Freemasonry renunciation prayer together. Later that afternoon, I was talking with someone who needed healing and found myself trying to minister deliverance to her, as I had just learned how to do three weeks before. She said it felt like she had a monkey on her back all the time. I prayed and commanded it to go in Jesus' name, trying to feign confidence that it would actually work. God touched her, and he healed her back.

Her chiropractor was perplexed the next day when she saw the healing. I was also amazed and remembered the word God had given me a few weeks before and the impartation prayer from Pablo Bottari a few weeks earlier. Wow! God had actually healed someone as I prayed for them! I thought to myself that the healing for someone else was really cool, but what about my brain tumor?

When I returned home from visiting family, my wife and I, our baby always in tow, began going to any and every meeting we could find where Jesus and only Jesus was preached and the anointing was present. We weren't sure what the anointing was even, but we figured that God seemed to be into it, and it had something to do with the Holy Spirit and healing, which was a good thing. I spent many hours studying every verse in the Bible that related in some way to healing and answered prayers, and I looked up the Hebrew and Greek meanings of key words. We spent more time daily than we ever had before praying, worshipping, fasting, and crying out to the Lord to help us.

We started reading books about how God heals. I read F. F. Bosworth's book *Christ the Healer*, which finally gave me a theological understanding of healing that provided a strong foundation for me. I really wrestled through that book. I read Norman Grubb's biography of Rees Howells, which gave me an altogether new vision for prayer and fasting. I read Bill Banks' autobiography which described his healing from terminal cancer, and, discovering that he was still alive some thirty years later and that he happened to live only a few miles away from us, we went to pay him a visit and ask for prayer.

One of the other books we read initially was Dutch Sheets' *Intercessory Prayer*. We read that God had actually healed someone as he prayed for them. We then heard he was coming to town as part of his 50-state tour. We thought, "Great, let's go hunt him down and get him to pray for us." So we went.

Dutch had just finished visiting four states in five days and, exhausted, snuck out right after the meeting. The conference organizers told us where his hotel was, so we went and tracked him down in his hotel lobby at 10:30 at night (not good conference etiquette, by the way). He was very nice and came down from his room to pray for us. "It will only take a minute or two," he assured us. At least fifteen minutes later, he helped carry my sorry, manifesting self into the car and cast out a few more demons for good measure, while I sat hunched over in the passenger seat.

We flew out early the next morning for Global Awakening's Voice of the Apostles (VOA) conference in Harrisburg, Pennsylvania. On the way, we took a side to trip to our old church in a neighboring state so that we could get more prayer. During this visit, my wife was experiencing debilitating pain in her back and shooting down her leg, making it all but impossible for her to carry around our three-month-old baby. This was a problem, given that we were on our way to a multi-day conference where I would be preoccupied seeking prayer for my healing.

My wife felt silly asking prayer for herself when I was clearly the one in urgent need, but she did ask. In fact, she received prayer three times the Sunday morning of our visit, without experiencing any benefit.

That evening, we met with a medical doctor friend of ours who happened to be halfway through a multi-week fast. She prayed for my wife for the fourth time that day. This doctor friend told us that she would often pray for her patients with back pain, and that she'd had a 100 percent healing rate after praying for about 75 patients.

As a doctor, she didn't have a lot of time to spend praying for her patients, so she'd worked out a kind of "deal" with the Lord for the healings to happen quickly.

She asked my wife whether one of her legs might be shorter than the other, pulled out a tape measure, and found that one leg was 3/8 of an inch shorter than the other. The doctor then prayed a thirty-second prayer, "Muscles, tendons, ligaments, grow out to the same length as the other leg in Jesus' name." I watched in amazement as my wife's leg gave a small lurch forward, and when we measured her legs a second time, they were the same length. I even tried to push the short leg back to its earlier length, but it wouldn't go. My wife got up and was amazed to discover that all the pain had instantly disappeared—and has never since returned.

Although we've subsequently heard of many similar "leg-lengthening" anecdotes and have even gotten to participate in a few of them, at the time we'd never heard of any such thing. This healing made a big impact on us. Although we still had to face the obviously larger problem of my tumor, our faith skyrocketed when God showed his love to us in this very practical way.

At VOA a few days later, I met Randy Clark for the first time. Seeing my wife carrying a baby to the prayer area and thinking the baby might need healing, he actually approached us. Here he was, the man at the center of everything; I felt so touched when he took time to pray for me.

At the same meeting I met Davi Silva, who, I was told, had been healed of Down's Syndrome. I almost couldn't believe that anyone could be healed of Down's (Remember, I'm a scientist). But then I saw the single palmar creases across Davi's hands and realized that he had the developmental signs of Down's syndrome, but he didn't actually have it. That blew me away. I asked Davi to pray for me for healing and impartation, especially in worship, since Davi is such an amazing worship leader, and I also lead worship. When he placed his hands on me, I felt the power of God so strongly that I shook violently on the floor for a long while. My wife stood by watching, not sure what to make of it all. By this time, she'd seen stranger things than this, so she wasn't fazed by just about anything! Afterwards, she said that my worship leading went up to a new level.

In the same meeting, Randy Clark kept talking about international ministry trips. I thought, "God, I don't have time for that. I've got to get healed first. Besides, it doesn't seem like a good idea to try to preach the Gospel and cast out demons in a communist country, especially if I have a life-threatening medical problem." Well, God kept bringing it up, so finally I started thinking about going to Cuba in early 2004 with Global Awakening. I started the application process, but still felt unsure.

During all of this, I kept getting regular MRIs of my head, every three months following the seizure. Right after the seizure, the radiologists said that the tumor could be one of several possible types, all of which are very bad. As a favor to a friend of ours who worked as a radiologist, the chief radiologist of the major research hospital where I'd been seen personally reviewed the films. He deflated any hope that the first radiologist had been over-zealous in his diagnosis. This was not a subtle anomaly, he assured us. About 90 percent of such enlargements turned out to be tumors and 10 percent passing inflammations, which would resolve themselves within a few months. The time window for such a resolution passed, and the mass remained.

After the first three months of powerful deliverance ministry and prayer for healing, I got another MRI. I had high hopes when I went for the scan. I'd felt the power of God so strongly. Surely I'd been healed. I even brought a video camera to the hospital so that my wife could film my expression as I opened up the envelope to see the good news. But the MRI said I wasn't any better, and that I still had the tumor. I was disappointed and confused. How could I not be healed after I had already received so much deliverance ministry and prayer for healing?

I had a choice to make. Fear or faith? Give up, or keep pursuing God with every ounce of strength within me? I decided that I would wrestle with God like Jacob did. I would spend more days and weeks fasting, more evenings in prayer, worship, and soaking in healing Scriptures. I would get more prayer from anointed ministries, and I would spend whatever time and money it cost, and go wherever I had to in order to get it. I really didn't have another option, except to get ready to die.

As the end of 2003 approached, I was praying on Saturday, a week before Christmas, and I sensed God telling me to visit a church with a specific name the next day. I hadn't heard of a church with that name, so I looked for it in the white pages. After quite a bit of searching, I found a nearby church by that name and figured out where it was. So we went the next morning. There were several hundred people gathered there. I didn't know anyone, but I said hello to the pastor for about 30 seconds and told him we were visiting—that was the extent of our conversation.

The service was great. The message was really encouraging. The pastor administered communion, and told us that Jesus poured out His blood for the forgiveness of our sins AND that Jesus gave His body for the healing of our diseases. That was the first time I ever heard that what Jesus did on the cross encompassed both salvation and healing. I was impressed with the power of this truth when the pastor asked those who were sick to hold up the bread and receive healing.

Many people were visiting that morning, and several responded to an altar call for salvation. Then suddenly at the end of the service, the pastor stopped everything and said that the Lord had just started speaking to him, and where was that guy with the five-month-old daughter who was visiting this morning? I figured there couldn't be too many of us, so I started walking forward.

The pastor then started prophesying over me. He said things like, "Wow, the Lord has a ride for you. Are you ready for a ride?" I said, "I'm as ready as I'm ever going to be." He went on and on about how the Lord had big plans for me. Later I told the prayer ministry team what was going on in my life, and they all prayed over me while the other three hundred or so in the service looked on. I never did go back to that church during the next several years, but I regarded them highly after that.

Right afterwards, we flew across the country to visit both of our extended families for Christmas. We ended up praying for many of our family members and ministering deliverance, which we had just learned how to do. In retrospect, perhaps we should have waited until we had ourselves experienced more complete freedom.

One of our relatives who was particularly oppressed wanted healing, but wasn't quite willing to renounce all the stuff that allowed the bondage to remain. We prayed for this person late at night on New Year's Eve. While we were praying, I felt an evil presence come into the room. We eventually stopped praying when it was clear we weren't getting anywhere. We still hadn't learned about doing "cleansing prayers," and we were exhausted. So we thoughtlessly stumbled off to bed, borrowing the bedroom of the person for whom we had just prayed. (The nightstand drawer by the bed even had some kind of idol in it that we didn't think to remove).

Early the next morning, my wife awoke with a start—something she'd done almost nightly since the seizure five months before—then she sank back onto her pillow, once again relieved that it was only the rain that had awakened her. Or was it this time?

I began to shake. I screamed. My mouth foamed. My eyes dilated and I was nonresponsive, as if I was neither awake nor asleep (Of course I don't remember any of this, but this is what my wife later told me). I was behaving just like I had during the first seizure.

But this time, instead of immediately reaching for the phone to dial 911, my wife began commanding the demons to leave me alone in Jesus' name. The parallels between the earlier "seizure" and what was now occurring and the scene in Mark 9 where the man brought his epileptic son to Jesus had not been lost on her. The worst of the episode soon passed, but as I still seemed rather out of it, my wife decided to call an ambulance just in case the paramedics could do anything useful. By the time they arrived, I was back to rights, and we sent them away, after agreeing to pick up a prescription for a low-dose anti-seizure medication. I hadn't taken any medicine for the past five months without any further seizures, and the timing of the second seizure seemed far from coincidental, but we were too exhausted to explain the finer points of demonology to the paramedics.

A few hours later we learned that, unbeknownst to us, another of our relatives had been ministering deliverance in that town for the past fifteen years, so we made an appointment for the following day. This individual didn't feel led to cast out any demons, but simply commanded them to come into the light of Jesus. That was a powerful command.

Three days later, we were back home, and I was leading worship for the same intercessory prayer group that had prayed during my first deliverance session. In the middle of worship, I slumped to the floor and started retching and had to run to the bathroom to vomit, even though I didn't feel sick. Apparently the demons had come into the light of Jesus, as commanded, and they didn't like it.

The person leading the prayer group remembered the name of the spirit from my wife's dream five months before and addressed it directly, and this led to a kind of final showdown. After another drawn-out, messy battle, I felt much better, although the other folks present complained of the foul sulfur smell left behind as the demons left. I was just glad to get rid of them after this renewed attack. In fact, this was the last prolonged deliverance session I was to undergo. What a beginning to the "ride" that had been prophesied over me.

Meanwhile, I heard about another healing meeting in Canada, so I got on a plane and flew there in mid-January, 2004. That is how it was during those months. Wherever I heard God was healing people, I would just get on a plane and go. I traveled many tens of thousands of miles in the year following the first seizure.

In Canada, I went to a luncheon where an evangelist prayed briefly over everyone present. Someone whispered in his ear that I had a brain tumor, so he—in full Pentecostal style—dramatically commanded the spirit of death to leave me! I went down with a thud, and something powerful seemed to be released.

Right after that, during the rest of the conference, I had a great time getting reacquainted with the Holy Spirit and felt very intoxicated as people in the meeting spent hours asking for more and more of the Holy Spirit. It was just like the first time I experienced the Holy Spirit in the UK in 1994. I was so excited that I called my wife at two in the morning to tell her how happy I felt. She responded that it was a good thing I didn't need to drive anywhere, because I sounded as if I would have been a hazard on the road! Once I "sobered" up a bit, I resumed pondering whether I should go to Cuba with Global

Awakening. As I was flying back through the Toronto airport, I unexpectedly found a Cuban five centavo coin in my wallet. I have no idea how it got there, but as soon as I saw it, I felt the power of God fall on me. "Okay, God, I get the message. I'll go to Cuba."

In late February of 2004, I went to Cuba (legally, I might add) with Global Awakening. I met Gary Oates, who was leading the trip, and who had been powerfully touched in Brazil just months earlier. During the first night in Cuba, Gary took my hands and prayed for impartation of gifts of healing. My left hand began to feel like it had hot sauce on it. I asked Gary what the burning sensation in my hands was, but it soon became obvious. From that day through the end of the week, I saw many people healed as I prayed for them, more than in my entire life before that. My world forever changed.

For instance, on the second day of the trip, there was a mostly-blind man walking with a cane outside one of the small churches where we were ministering. After he received his sight, he was eager to pray to receive Jesus and to renounce his involvement in the occult. I remembered having spent many hours in my college days doggedly handing out tracts and feeling frustrated when no one seemed to get saved through my efforts. When God revealed His love by healing, evangelism became easy. People actually wanted to become Christians!

There was another woman that same day in Cuba who came to a church service very weak and emaciated, with an obviously distended abdomen. Doctors had sent her home to die from ovarian cancer. She was depressed and fatalistic about her condition, since others in her family had died from cancer. At a certain point I stopped translating the team's prayers (since I was one of the few team members who spoke Spanish, I served as one of the translators). We began to address the lying spirits that were speaking death over her. We prayed in English and told the lying spirits to get off her and shut up in Jesus' name. Then we suggested that she sit down in the church service and soak in the Lord's presence.

About fifteen minutes later, we heard a scream. The Holy Spirit had fallen on the woman so powerfully that she was knocked backward. When she got up, the tumor had disappeared, her husband was crying with joy, and the woman was jumping up and down with excitement and supernatural strength, despite the fact that she could hardly stand up by herself just moments before.

As it turned out, a family crisis forced Gary and his wife Kathy to go home earlier than planned from the Cuba trip, leaving our team without leadership for the last few days. The rest of us thought that we were done ministering at this point, but were we ever wrong! It was so encouraging to discover that God really could work through "ordinary" Christians like us, even without the presence of anointed leaders.

Perhaps the most powerful night of the whole trip took place after the Oates had departed, and we had gone to our final city of the trip. A few of us found a random church of about three hundred members. We just went out wandering on a Sunday afternoon and found this church a few blocks from our hotel, knocked on the door, and ended up talking to the pastor. He invited us to come back that night to share, and, when we did, he felt led to turn the service over to us. We began with some testimonies, then the team members had words of knowledge. By the end of the service, around midnight, just about everyone who needed it had experienced healing, including many with longstanding vision problems.

I also found that I really enjoyed ministering deliverance to people and seeing them set free. I didn't mind the manifestations, because I was so grateful to have received deliverance myself. Besides that, all of these deliverances were pretty mild compared to my own

(I always try to focus on loving the person when I minister and avoid unnecessary manifestations, following Pablo Bottari's advice).

Some deliverances seemed to have come right out of a script from the New Testament. One woman I ministered to on a subsequent trip to Uganda in 2005 said she had "witchcraft" and wanted to get rid of it. I started praying, and she started manifesting a demon. She fell over, closed her eyes, screamed, and convulsed. The demons screamed through her "Don't touch me!" But I kept my hand on her head and commanded them to come out. After a few moments, the demons screamed, "We are many!" through her in a strange voice. So I said, "I don't care; all of you come out in Jesus' name." She kept manifesting, and the next one said "She's my wife!" I said, "No, she's not; I cancel that demonic marriage covenant in Jesus' name. She is the bride of Christ, so come out now in Jesus' name!" After a few more manifestations, she was in a heap on the floor praising and thanking Jesus for setting her free. "Thank you Jesus!" she kept repeating. Deliverance has since become a significant part of my ministry.

In March through May of 2004, I flew across the country at least three times, going to different healing meetings. At one point we drove 5,000 miles (think: baby in car) in the span of three weeks, tracking down the anointing.

Sometimes people ask me what "faith" is. My personal definition of faith is that it's 90 percent unwillingness to give up and the willingness to persevere in pressing in for more of God's healing presence. If you have enough faith to keep asking for prayer (not just praying for yourself, which is important too), you have enough faith to be healed.

As a side note: I think that "positive confession" teachings can sometimes get out of hand and induce an unnecessary element of fear of making a negative confession—especially when linked with a bizarre unwillingness to pray for someone more than once lest this suggest a lack of faith. In fact, I think it takes *more* faith to pray repeatedly. It's important to avoid the hurtful tendency to blame those not yet healed for presumed lack of faith or holiness. Nevertheless, there is something to speaking words of life rather than death, breaking word curses, and refusing to "own" diagnoses and prognoses that contradict the promises of the Word of God. When contending for healing, some things are better left unsaid, while Scriptural promises are always worth proclaiming.

Now I didn't always *feel* super-confident that I would be healed. For months I really thought I was going to die. But I resolved in my spirit, and expressed through my actions, the determination to clutch the hem of Christ's garment and not let go, no matter what. Of course, God *can* heal you right in your living room, and sometimes does just that. But it seems that God often does meet people in special ways when they make costly, sacrificial efforts to go wherever necessary to seek out prayer.

I've often thought of Matthew 11:12 in this regard, "From the days of John the Baptist until now, the kingdom of heaven has been forcefully advancing, and forceful men lay hold of it."[23]

As I forcefully pursued the healing presence of God, I received prayer repeatedly in the same meetings where the people next to me were having metal plates dissolve and missing bones recreated. Now that really boosted my faith! At one conference, we watched as God instantaneously—and quite dramatically—healed a fourteen-year-old friend of ours of life-long asthma and allergies. A few years later, she won a track scholarship to college!

God also sent a variety of people our way, seemingly just to en-

[23] NIV

courage us by speaking detailed prophetic words over us and sharing apt testimonies. For example, a woman showed up one week (for the first and only time) at the city-wide intercessory prayer group that we had made our home, just to testify of having been instantaneously healed of a brain tumor while watching the movie *The Passion*.

As various people prayed for me on different occasions, I felt the power of God hit me repeatedly. I shook like I'd hugged an electrical pole, got laid out for hours, had gold dust appear on me, and got all kinds of teaching and impartation to equip me to minister healing to others. Just about every nationally prominent itinerant healing evangelist prayed for me at least once during this period—Mahesh Chavda, James Maloney, Bill Johnson, Benny Hinn and several others, as well as many "ordinary" Christians. I also received prayer from ministries like Cleansing Streams and various healing rooms—often with dramatic effects. Each of these encounters would be a story in itself. I figured the impartation was a nice bonus, but my main concern was still my own healing.

Six months after the first seizure, I got another MRI. The doctors said they still saw a mass, but it wasn't growing. They were no longer as sure exactly what it was, since they had expected some growth. Even so the doctors told us to expect significant growth within the next few months, and asked if we wouldn't like to consider surgery.

After nine months, they did another MRI and said it still wasn't growing, whatever "it" was. In fact, they thought maybe it even looked a little smaller. After 12 months, the MRI reports, which thereafter were ordered at progressively longer intervals, silently dropped the word tumor. The doctors never did jump up and down shouting, "Hallelujah, you're heeeeealed, brother!" But what they didn't say spoke volumes.

After a year of intense prayer ministry and regular MRIs, the doctors basically said there's nothing of interest to see here, and we don't need to see you for a while, so go away. Interestingly, a few months before the doctors stopped talking about tumors, my wife visited the Spokane Healing Rooms, where a team prophesied that we would get our medical documentation of the manifestation of my healing, but that the doctors would not recognize it.

I cannot point to a single moment at which I was sure I was healed, although I can point to a series of highly significant moments when the Holy Spirit ministered powerfully through the prayers of specific individuals. It is the Lord alone who gets the glory for my healing, the Lord chose to work through the loving prayers of a number of His faithful servants.

At a certain point, my wife and I felt confident enough to have a second child. Her middle name is "Anastasia," meaning "resurrection," because the Lord has graciously given us our lives back. But we no longer feel that they are *our* lives, but His.

When my wife and I were married ten years ago, we felt led to select a rather odd wedding Scripture, John 12:24, "I tell you the truth, unless a kernel of wheat falls to the ground and dies, it remains only a single seed. But if it dies, it produces many seeds."[24] This has truly been our experience. As I write this, it has been nearly six years since the original diagnosis, and I have been totally symptom-free for more than five years, with no medical treatment for the tumor except prayer ministry. Moreover, God launched me and my wife into a healing and deliverance ministry, and we have seen all kinds of miracles and deliverances since that time.

After I returned from Cuba in March 2004, the people at Global Awakening said that if I thought the trip to Cuba was good, then I

[24] NIV

would really enjoy going to Brazil. So in September of 2004, I traveled to Brazil with Randy Clark. Near the beginning of the trip in Belem, Randy was ministering impartation. When he laid his hands on me, I felt the power of God again.

After I received prayer for impartation, I went and got in line again for a double helping. My hand began to shake as Randy prayed for me a second time, and he simply said, "I bless the power in that hand." A few hours later that night, at the soccer stadium, I experienced the most powerful night of ministry I have ever had. I saw God do many miracles as I prayed for people in the name of Jesus.

For the first time that night, I saw two totally blind people—brothers, perhaps 8 and 11 years of age—receive their eyesight right in front of me as I prayed for them. That really wrecked me. That same night I saw tumors dissolve as I prayed, and all kinds of pain left—almost 100 percent of the people I prayed for got healed.

During Global's international trips, people often talk about "taking it [the impartation] back home with you." After I got back home from Brazil, I told the pastors of my (new) church about what had happened, and they invited me to take a few minutes to share in the service on Sunday morning. So I got up and passionately described all the wonderful miracles I had seen right in front of me, and how God had healed so many people.

It was all downhill from there! Right after the service, people came up and wanted me to pray for them, so I did, and several were healed. Then I got permission to have people in the church who had been healed give their testimonies up front on Sunday mornings. The pastors invited me to come up for a few minutes the next week, and then the next, and so it continued. From that day on, there was an outbreak of miracles and healings that started in the church and went on for a couple of years, until we moved out of state.

We trained up a prayer ministry team, and people were healed of years of pain and lifelong conditions: vision and hearing were restored, cancers inexplicably disappeared, short legs lengthened instantaneously, and the brokenhearted received inner healing and deliverance. We especially saw healings when our pastor allowed time during the service for those healed in previous weeks to give their testimonies and then opened up an opportunity for further prayer ministry.

In all of this, while I was running off to healing meetings, God prospered my scientific career greatly. I made scientific discoveries that made national and international news. There even came a time when I had to turn down opportunities to help run healing meetings because I had to go to Washington, D.C., to brief national security agencies on my research. I didn't expect to face this kind of dilemma a year before, but I tried to "seek first the Kingdom," and sure enough, the rest was added to me.

Around Christmas in 2004, three months after I returned from my first trip to Brazil, I flew across the country to visit family. While I was there, a relative invited some friends to hear my stories of miracles and healings from Brazil. I began to tell about the blind and lame people who were healed. After that, one of the people there began to cry, saying he had a tumor growing on his stomach and was scared. I did some deliverance ministry for him, then prayed for healing of the tumor. He got up to leave, and before he reached the front door of the house, he felt his stomach and realized that the tumor was almost completely gone. I checked back a few weeks later, and his wife reported that it had not returned. He and his wife went on their way rejoicing, and seeing the miracle happen had a lasting impact on my family members who were present. One of my own relatives who was there immediately turned away from years of involvement in the New Age, realizing that "It finally makes sense; it's Jesus who does the healing."

Around this time, the Lord continued to increase the gifts of healing and deliverance in our lives. I had begun volunteering at the same healing rooms where I initially got deliverance ministry myself, and every week we saw people with all kinds of illnesses and bondages get free. Chronic pain left, vision was restored, and many stubborn demons were kicked out in Jesus' name.

One time someone came in who was severely demonized as a result of having very high Freemasons in the family. She went into a trance, stopped breathing, and otherwise manifested severely as we began the Freemasonry renunciation. But after we had gently ministered for a couple of hours in love, she got a lot of freedom and left full of joy (Unfortunately, the new person ministering with me got freaked out by the manifestations and quit).

On another occasion, several of us answered a call to pray for a woman kept tied up in a psychiatric ward. After we visited several times, she was released from the hospital. Then, after weeks of additional ministry, she was able to go off her medications without problems. In the following months, she became a regular volunteer at the healing rooms and helped minister freedom to many others.

Another day in January 2005, after I got back from the trip to Brazil, I went to pick up my child from daycare. As I talked about healings and miracles with the director at the daycare center, her husband came up and mentioned that he had had severe gout for a long time. I took him aside and took authority over it, breaking it off in Jesus' name. He said that he felt hot, and instantly the pain left. He said he hadn't been so sure about the healing thing, but now that he was healed, he was convinced, and very grateful. I saw him regularly for more than a year after that. Whenever he saw me, he thanked me again for praying for him, whereupon I said we should thank the Lord for healing him. This was our regular greeting.

I've had a number of similar opportunities to minister to people in non-church settings like homes and offices. For instance, a computer repairman came to my office one day, complaining of back pain from a pinched sciatic nerve. I asked him if he'd like me to pray for him. At first he ignored me and went about repairing my computer. However, he kept on complaining about the pain, so I asked again if I could pray, and this time he agreed. I prayed a thirty second prayer and asked how he felt. He seemed surprised and said his back felt much better. I then asked whether he knew Jesus, and he said that he had been raised in a church, but he had backslidden. I got to talk with him about the Father's love, and he was touched.

Of course, not every prayer ministry opportunity is easy. Randy Clark has a sermon series on the agony of defeat and the thrill of victory in praying for healing. In May of 2005, an elderly man in our church, who had himself been an influential local leader in the early charismatic movement, was diagnosed with terminal cancer. I went over to his house repeatedly and prayed extensively over him on various occasions. Then he died.

I was sad and angry after that. I gathered our prayer group and we prayed in light of Exodus 22. This passage states that when the thief is caught, he has to restore at least double what was stolen. We prayed and fasted for days after that, asking God to give us at least two cancer healings as payback for the enemy's stealing of the life of this precious brother.

A week or two later, I had to get some immunizations in preparation for a mission trip to Uganda. I saw the same nurse who had given me shots for Brazil a year earlier. She was friendly and asked how my last trip went, so I started talking about all the miracles. She listened intently. After nearly an hour, she asked if I would be willing to pray for her elderly mother, who was just outside the office. She explained that her mother had an artificial knee that was now painful and making popping sounds, and the doctors were thinking of operating again. The mother came in just as the nurse went out to get my shots. I explained to the mother how Isaiah 53 addresses healing as well as forgiveness, and then I prayed for healing. All the pain left her, and after another prayer, the popping in her knee stopped. The nurse came back in with my shots and asked me how the prayer went. I suggested she go ask her mother. The nurse went out to talk with her mother briefly, then came back in and asked me if I would pray for her, too. So I again explained Isaiah 53 and prayed for the nurse right in her medical office. She had had a painful problem with her ankle for two years. After I prayed, all the pain left, and then I went around the whole clinic, looking for others who needed healing.

When I got back to my office that same afternoon, I had a message waiting for me. It was from a member of our church. She had had a cancer spread to another location after the original tumor had been removed, and I had prayed for her in church two days before. She was reporting on her visit to her doctor that day. The medical staff had anesthetized her, but after doing one last scan, they realized that the new lump had unexpectedly disappeared in the last few days. So, with some consternation, the doctors told her simply to wait for the anesthetic to wear off, and then she could go home. The woman was elated. I asked her to share her testimony in church the next Sunday, and by the time Sunday came, we had another testimony of cancer being healed prior to medical intervention. So, within a month of losing one church member to cancer, we had two cancer healing testimonies shared publicly during church. This didn't negate the pain caused by our other brother's death, but we remembered the promise the Lord gave David in 1 Samuel 30:8, "pursue, overtake, and recover all."[25] In his faithfulness, God gave our church two cancer healings shortly after the enemy had stolen a

---

[25] Excerpted from KJV

brother from us, just as He says in Exodus 22.

In August 2005, I received another impartation that took me from ministering healing individually to preaching and ministering healing to crowds. Earlier that summer I had led a small healing meeting. I taught a breakout session on healing at a Christian conference, and a few people were healed of some pain when I prayed en masse over the crowd. That was good, but nothing like the level of power I had seen in Brazil.

Then I heard that Randy Clark was doing a meeting at a small church a few states away, so my wife and I, along with some friends, took a road trip to the meeting. On a Saturday night, I was sitting in the back of the church there. Randy prayed for the Holy Spirit to come, and as he did so, my mouth began to twitch. It was an unusual sensation, like there was a power in my mouth, and I could hardly contain the urge to move my mouth and lips all over the place. A few moments after that, Randy said that some people would begin to feel something in their mouths. "That's me," I thought to myself. Randy said that people with that sensation should come forward for more prayer and impartation, so I went forward. When he got to me, I asked him, "What is this?" He just looked at me and smiled and said something like "more." I don't remember much beyond that, except that I fell out intoxicated and rolled around on the floor laughing hysterically for several hours, while my wife looked on.

That was Saturday night. Sunday morning after church, we heard there was a reunion for a school for the deaf at the lake a few miles away. "Excellent," I thought. So we and our friends who had come to the meeting with us all went down to the lake and found lots of deaf people to pray for, and one reported some hearing improvement. Then we drove back home, and that very night, just one day after the impartation, I led a meeting for the youth group in our church. I preached with new power and conviction. During the meeting, I was amazed to see how many young people had chronic, even lifelong conditions. I preached from Isaiah 53, that Jesus forgives sins and heals diseases. Then I took authority over all sickness in the room in Jesus' name, and we prayed for healing.

The next week, I came back for the second half of the two-week series, and we heard testimonies from the young people who had been prayed for the previous week during the meeting. Many had received powerful healings, even from lifelong conditions. It was one of the first and most powerful healing services I have led, considering the type of healings and percentage of people healed.

Since that time, if I have just one opportunity to preach, I speak from Isaiah 53 about forgiveness of sins and healing of diseases. I have preached this message now across the U.S., on several return trips to Brazil and in Africa, and the Lord has powerfully healed people everywhere. He is so faithful!

Between ministry trips, my wife and I continued to work as university professors. We moved to another state when the Lord worked things out to give us even better jobs with more Kingdom opportunities. Randy Clark was doing a conference at our church when we received news of our appointments, and he felt led to hold a public commissioning for us during the Sunday morning service, saying that we were being sent as forerunners, bringing the gospel into the universities.

Within a week after we moved, we met a church full of people, many of them affiliated with the university, very hungry for the presence of God and healing. By the end of our first month in town, we were teaching another multi-week training class in our home with our new pastor in attendance and launching a new prayer ministry team. After that, we began to host regular soaking prayer meetings and to lead healing services, teach basic and advanced healing and deliverance training (which people come from hours away to take), and preach occasionally. We also started healing rooms, first out of our house, and then through another area church. We've had a number of opportunities to minister to college students, professors, and university staff members.

Whenever we have the chance, we still love to take time off to travel and participate in what God is doing around the world. During a visit to Heidi and Rolland Baker's ministry in Mozambique, Africa, in 2009, we stood just feet away as the Lord healed one person after another person of severe hearing and visual impairments. We were even able to use our scholarly training to measure and document these improvements with an audiometry machine and vision charts.

One young man had never heard or spoken before in his entire life, but a few minutes after healing prayer, he was repeating words and sounds that he could now hear. Another young man who came for prayer had severe vision problems. There weren't even any "anointed" healing evangelists around, just a few of us ordinary Christians. Within a few minutes, the young man, who before prayer could not read the top line of an eye chart (20/400) was reading the 20/125 line. After a few more minutes of prayer, he could read the 20/40 line, which is quite fine print. After that, he and a number of onlookers who had witnessed this miracle were eager to pray to receive Jesus as Savior and then ran to catch up with the group that had just gone to a nearby river to be baptized.

When we first started ministering to people in our home, people came who had heard of us by word-of-mouth and drove for hours to get to us, desperately looking for help, and we often ministered as many as five evenings a week. However, we would frequently seem to get "stuck" mid-way through a challenging deliverance. It would be obvious to all that some evil presence had been exposed and was almost—but not quite—on its way out. Another turning point for us was a Global Awakening healing school in January 2007 in a neighboring state, to which we took a number of folks from our new church. After this conference, we started to see breakthroughs in ministering deliverance much more quickly and easily.

One of the people we took with us to the healing school was a college student we'd never met before. She'd happened to visit our church the week before the healing school. It turned out she had been depressed and chronically ill for years and even remembered seeing demons in her room when she was still in her crib. We prayed for her once after returning from the healing school, and we still got stuck. We decided to take a few days to fast and pray before meeting again, and when we met a second time, we scarcely had to pray for five minutes before she was totally free. Since then, she has literally been brimming with joy, health, passion, and anointing. She's seen many other college students healed, saved, and delivered, and infiltrated hard-to-reach "New-Agey" settings with the Gospel. Her parents also visited and received ministry, training, and anointing to minister to hurting populations back in their home town.

Prayer and fasting certainly played a role in this young woman's freedom, but we also noticed that her's was one of a number of breakthroughs that came within a few weeks of the January 2007 healing school. More often than not after that, people who came to our house for prayer, weighed down by the oppression of the enemy, left at the end of the evening with joyful countenances, having had their burdens lifted. We always try to minister gently in love and keep the demonic manifestations to a minimum.

We could tell a lot more stories of how we've seen the Lord set other people free and then launch them into influential ministries of their own. We continue to see all kinds of healings, and our lives are wonderfully full in ways that we wouldn't have imagined before I had the brain tumor and got healed. God took our worst nightmare, defeated the enemy, and turned the whole thing into the greatest blessing of our lives. We affirm the words of 1 Corinthians 15: 57, "But thanks be to God! He gives us the victory through our Lord Jesus Christ."[26]

---

[26] NIV

Pete and Jenna[27]
Called Out and Raised Up for Asia

Our story is really very simple. Unexpectedly, God touched us in a service one day, and we were changed forever. He called us to spend our lives loving the forgotten. And He has empowered us to do that.

We once lived a normal life in the U.S., raising two healthy boys, enjoying promising careers. From a spiritual point of view, we were very nominal Christians, in that we had been Christians all of our lives. Peter was raised in the Baptist church, and I was raised in the Church of God. I always say that I was more of a detriment to the body of Christ than I was a gift. I didn't bear any fruit. I was a contradiction. I believed one way, but lived another way. We even questioned our salvation, although we believed, if you had asked us, that Jesus was the Son of God. But we had absolutely no fruit to show for our beliefs.

We attended Suncoast Worship Center where Tom Jones was pastoring. Tom likes to say we were the last ones in on Sunday and the first ones out the door. We did the Sunday morning drive-thru,

---

[27] Names and some places changed for security reasons.

but we had a yearning for more. There had always been a yearning in both of our hearts for more of the Lord. We knew that there was more, but we just didn't know how to find it. Spiritually we were lazy, but we were also *hungry*.

Pete worked as a loan officer at a bank, and I was a speech language pathologist. I had worked very hard to get my credentials—seven years of university study, including a master's degree in communicative disorders, as well as a year of clinical fellowship. I loved my job, and I loved my kids and being home with them.

Pete and I were both very successful. We had a nice house with a swimming pool and two nice cars. We were really living the American dream. We had our family with us, and we had our two small children. We were in good health, but there was much lacking. Because of that, we were seeking, but we didn't even know how to seek. The Holy Spirit was so kind to lead us to where we needed to be. But we were not seeking ministry. No, I always said, I never wanted to be a pastor's wife. I would do anything, but I never wanted to be a pastor's wife. It never seemed like a fun job to me.

In January 2000, we had been attending Suncoast Worship Center in Englewood, Florida for a few years. I had been raised in that church. I remember walking in while Randy was having revival meetings. I think it was a Friday night, and we hadn't been at the earlier sessions. Several people in my family had gone, and I remember my mom saying, "You and Pete should really think about going tonight." I think it might have been the last night that Randy was there. She repeated, "You guys should really think about going tonight," and we just fluffed it off and didn't think too much about it. Mom pursued it and said, "You go, and I'll watch the kids for you." We said okay, mostly because we had heard some things that were going on, and we were a little interested. When we got there, the church was completely packed. There were people standing in the aisles. We had never had people hungry like that at our church before.

There were maybe 500 people there; it was a small church. The gentleman who met us at the door obviously didn't recognize us. He didn't know he was speaking prophetically when he said, "Oh, you guys must be pastors." We said "No, we're not," but he was not listening to us and took us right to the front and sat us on the very front row which was reserved for pastors. We had said, "We're not," but there were no other seats available. Normally, we would have had to go to an overflow room. God must have just known that. I don't even know if this man knows this, but that phrase was something we heard over and over again after that night. "Oh, you must be pastors...oh, you must be pastors." We'd say, "No, we're not!" This was before the Lord revealed His plan for our lives and changed our hearts. That night we simply walked in, and He sat us up front.

We were just mesmerized by Randy and his stories, by the purity of his heart. I remember thinking that he had eyes like Jesus, and I had never seen anybody like that before. I'd never seen anybody care so much through their eyes. It was just very sweet. That drew us.

Honestly, I don't even remember what the service was about. I don't have any recollection of the message or anything. But I remember when he gave the altar call, I knew that I had to be up there. Pete and I held hands, went up together, and stood right in the middle. We just grabbed each other's hand and went. I think I was surprised at Pete's willingness to go with me. Randy just went down the line and prayed for people. I mean, it was really simple. It was just "More, Lord." I had never been slain in the Spirit before, but we fell down under the power of the Holy Spirit. I remember Pete standing over me, crying, and he kept saying that I looked just like an angel. He had never been "spiritual" before. He'd never been touched like that. He knew something was happening, but he didn't know what. I remember getting up and thinking to myself, "Everything's changed."

I remember waking up the next morning, and Pete and I saying to each other that we were completely different. It wasn't anything that we had to do, like "Okay, let's go study our Bibles together." Our hearts were completely taken over by the Lord.

I remember sitting in my black rocking chair at home, where I used to rock and feed my babies, devouring the Bible. I read all the books that I could get my hands on and went anywhere I could to hear more about Jesus. Sometimes, I wonder if that was a salvation moment or simply the infilling of the Holy Spirit because I thought that I really believed, but there was no fruit in my life. Afterwards, I was a completely new person. Even memories from my past disappeared. I have very, very vague memories of any sin in my life. People ask me about when I was younger, and I have a really hard time remembering any of the "yucky" stuff. Before that time, I was always revisiting old memories.

We really didn't sense a call to missions at first. In fact, I remember Pete telling me that the first time he heard someone have an altar call for missions, he said, "Thank you, God, that You didn't call me to missions." However, we had a prophecy from Bob Johnson, Bill Johnson's brother, on our first mission trip, nine months after we were touched. He prophesied right on the money. He said that he saw us going to the mission field, and he saw us in heaven with all these children around me calling me Mama.

I thought he was wrong. I really thought he was wrong. I was sitting next to a close friend. She had grown up with a heart for missions, and I really, really thought he was getting the connection crossed. I didn't say anything, but I just thought, "No, you must be hearing for my friend, not for me." Going into missions was never a desire of our hearts—the farthest thing from it.

We were both surprised when we felt led to go to Brazil for the first time on a two-week mission trip. That seemed like such a big step- two weeks! I remember our family thinking that we were crazy. I know some of them thought that we had gotten involved with a cult. It was such a radical transformation, especially because healing was involved. A lot of people thought that we had lost our marbles.

Our trip was one of the first mission trips for Global Awakening. One night on the trip, they split up into teams, and we were assigned to go with Bill Johnson—no one knew who he was at that time. We were disappointed not to be with Randy, but after one night with Bill, we said, "Oh, my goodness, who is this man?" He was amazing! It was a small team, a small trip, yet we remember so much happening in Brazil. We didn't know anything about anything, but here we were on a mission trip, ministering to others, with so much being downloaded and given to us as well. It was amazing.

Then one night, Bob Johnson took a team of four women to go out on the streets of Sao Paulo, Brazil, to minister to the prostitutes. I did not want to go because I was afraid. He came to me and Valerie and said, "I feel like you're supposed to be two of the four." I was just scared to pieces. I'd never won anybody to the Lord. In fact, I'd never witnessed to anybody about the Lord before I had been touched. Since January I'd been talking about the Lord, but not anything like this.

He said, "You pray about it and let me know if you want to do this." I did pray about it, and I knew that I was supposed to go out on the street. I remember him walking us through it. He sent Valerie and me and one interpreter out on the street and said, "Be careful, because if there are pimps, they have guns. It can be a little dangerous, but go and bring flowers to the women." So we just got a bunch of roses; we went and brought flowers to the prostitutes, and we spoke to them from our hearts. I remember this was a pivotal moment because I was standing there handing a flower to this one woman whose face I can still picture, and I felt like there was a tunnel of love that came from heaven to earth. I felt like I had a baptism of love, like I was completely immersed in the love of God. I loved that woman like she was my daughter.

I was just beside myself. Many women got saved—I don't remember how many. It was such a powerful moment for me, and I remember thinking to myself that I would never be the same. I knew that I had waffled back and forth in the past, so I couldn't just say that I would never be the same again. Over time, people have a tendency to forget experiences and return to their old ways. I was afraid that even though I felt I could never be the same, unless I *did* something and continued to operate in this new love, I, too, would lose the fire and passion and would return to life as usual. This thought really scared me.

I said, "God, you have to show me the poor," because where we live there weren't any poor people. It was a very affluent place, so God needed to show me the poor people. I told Him that I didn't want to lose it. I was just crying out, "I don't want to lose this." I had just discovered that what I had been given was what I was created to do. It was so easy, and I wasn't afraid of anything except losing my new passion.

We went back the next day and met with these women and some of their children. We spent time with them on the street and brought them gifts. When we left, they cried and we cried. Then we kept in contact with them. We had done more than just minister to them; now we had a relationship with them. This is the Kingdom.

After we returned home, we were not the same people. We began seeking to serve in love in our neighborhood. One night, Pete and I were fixing dinner, and I had something in the oven. I felt like the Lord said, "It's time to go." So I made a peanut butter and jelly sandwich, got a bottle of water, and a cookie and put it in a brown paper bag. I brought five lunches in total. We had about an hour and a half until dinner was done, and I felt like the Lord told me, "I want you to go down by the beach."

Pete and I got in the car with kids. We strapped the kids in and went down to the beach looking for the homeless or anybody who was in need. We didn't see anybody. We circled around, and we didn't see anybody. I thought, "Well, I must have missed it." But as we were leaving the parking lot, I felt like the Lord said, "Turn around and go again." We went back around, and in the woods by the beach, I saw a little flicker of light. It was a little campfire, and there were homeless people in the woods—five of them.

We cut through the woods, and I didn't know what to do, so I just said, "I thought you might be hungry. Jesus loves you." I was very nervous, so I said again, "Jesus loves you." They asked, "Are you an angel?" I said, "No, I'm not an angel. Jesus loves you, and He doesn't want you to be hungry. He sent me to bring you some food." It was our first step in the States to begin reaching out to the ones no one else sees.

From that point on, God began showing us where to go, because we didn't know where the poor were. He said, "They might not be in your town, but they could be in surrounding towns, so you'll have to drive a little bit." For this reason, we started going to day labor places. These are places where people go to get work for a day, and then they get paid for that day. They start lining up at 4:30 in the morning, because the people who get there first get the jobs first. Many we met were on drugs, were drunk, or were prostitutes. Some were just trying to make ends meet, but all of them were lonely and hurting.

We just started getting up really early in the morning on Tuesdays, and we would make these little bag lunches and bring bottles of water. We would go sit with the poor out in the parking lots behind these alleys while it was still dark. For three years, we would drive to Sarasota, which was an hour away. We would go every week, and we would just sit with the people.

We saw more miracles on the street than I had ever seen in my entire life. I remember one time when we were out on the street. There was a man, and he had been drunk every time we had been there. We prayed for him every time. He would just come back the same way the next week, and he wasn't being changed. Then one day he came and said that he had this huge cancer in his throat. You could see it; there was a ball (tumor) right there. We asked, "Can we pray for you?" His marriage was a wreck. His wife had left him, and he was estranged from his children, but he said we could pray. Valerie and I prayed for him, and he left.

Then the next week we didn't see him and the week after that we didn't see him. I didn't know what had happened to him. Four weeks later, I was sitting inside the building talking to a 17-year-old boy who was just a wreck, and I was sharing with him about the love of Jesus. Because he seemed so interested, I asked him after I shared with him, "Are you ready to become a Christian?" He said, "No! I'm really not ready." "That's okay," I said. "Can I pray that the Lord would get you ready? If what I'm saying about Jesus is true, would you want to know?" He said, "Yeah." I said, "Can I pray that the Lord would get you ready?" And he said, "Yeah, you can pray that." I just said, "God, get him ready in Jesus' name. Amen." It was just a really simple prayer.

So I walked outside, and the same man who we had prayed for four weeks before came running up in front of everyone. He was saying, "Look at my neck, look at my neck!" He said, "Right after you guys prayed for me (I believe he said it was the next day) I woke up, and it was completely gone." He had gone back to the doctor, and they had cleared him. No more cancer. It was gone! He had been restored to his marriage, and his children wanted a relationship with him again. He was telling this story to everybody in the middle of the night in this back alley. He was saying, "Jesus heals, Jesus heals." He was clean physically, too. Often demonic presence manifests itself in people through uncleanness. He smelled good; he was clean and hadn't been drinking. He was sharing about his testimony with everyone. He was freed from everything. He was dressed nicely, and I think he told us he was going on an interview that day. He had to come back to tell us.

I got so excited. I got up on a box and said, "Did you hear the testimony?" I had never been that bold before. I said, "Jesus healed this man." I began to tell them the story and said, "If you're sick, you need to come, because Jesus will heal you. You know we're going to pray for you." So I prayed for some people, and I went to the van to get more sandwiches, turned around and here's the 17-year-old boy from inside standing right in front of me. He said, "My throat's on fire. I've had an infection, and I don't have money for an antibiotic." He said it again, "My throat is on fire. I just heard about that man being healed. Can you pray for me?" I said, "Oh, I'd just love to pray for you," and I said a simple, "Lord, heal him in Jesus' name." He just started weeping because he got healed. I looked at him, and I sensed the change. I asked him, "Are you ready now?" He got right down on his knees in front of me, had his hands lifted up, and he gave his life to the Lord.

Those testimonies happened all the time on the streets. We would hear radical testimonies of healing, salvation and deliverance.

I was really thankful for that time.

Right after the trip to Brazil, I went to the first Voice of the Apostles conference in St. Louis. I remember I really felt led to go on that trip, and it was right after we had gotten back. Now, I had little babies at home, but I was just so desperate. Pete couldn't go because he had to work. There were only about 200 people, I think, at the conference. There was Heidi Baker, Bill Johnson, Randy Clark, and Henry Madaba; I remember listening to everyone and thinking, "Oh, my goodness." I was getting radically fed and was being radically changed. I still remember listening to Heidi Baker. A friend who was with me nudged me, because Heidi was having a call for people giving their life to missions. She said, "Jenna, that's you!" I said, "No, that's not me." I had listened very carefully to the cost because Heidi, at that time, had talked about the cost. She said, "This is not for everyone." She had talked about her children and the sacrifice of going on the mission field. She talked about suffering and the cost of following Jesus. I had such a fear of the Lord.

I really think it was a good thing that I didn't go forward, that I wasn't willing to go to the front just to get prayer from Heidi. I knew that if I went up, God would do it. I said. "No." I could see myself on the mission field, but I didn't want to endanger my children. I had not been able to give my kids to the Lord.

As I am revisiting this, it is now 2010, and I am sitting in an Asian hospital caring for my son who just came out of surgery after suffering from second and third degree burns on the mission field. Yes, there is a cost!

The following year, just nine months later, Randy went on another trip to Brazil, and we went with him. We were radically touched again. Pete was completely miserable at his job, completely unsatisfied. He was still doing well, but he would sit out in the parking lot before he went into work, just not wanting to go inside. I remember him telling me that he would read his Bible and cry in the parking lot of the bank and say, "God use me, use me." But neither of us knew what else we could do. We weren't pastors; we couldn't go into ministry. At least that's what we thought.

On our second trip to Brazil, Tom Jones, then the senior pastor of Suncoast Worship Center, sensed that we were supposed to come on staff. We didn't know anything about anything, but Tom and his wife Brenda saw something that God was doing inside us. We weren't ordained; we weren't anything. But I remember Pastor Tom pulling Pete and me aside one morning and asking if we had ever considered being in ministry fulltime. I remember Pete crying and saying he had. Tom gave him many reasons why you wouldn't want to go into ministry, all the hard stuff. He just laid it all out. Pete was crying and saying it would be such an honor. If we could do this for our whole life, if we could give our whole life, it would be an honor. The next morning Randy told Pete that prior to his conversation with Tom, when Randy had prayed for him, he felt a strong word that God was calling him to leave his job to go into fulltime ministry.

Every time anybody would come to our church, it didn't matter where we were sitting, Pete and I would always be called out. They would pick us out to prophesy over us. I remember that Patricia King prophesied over us that we were in a whirlwind. Man, she hit it right on with everything that she said about children and that we would be transitioning and winds of change were coming. She was just all over us.

Randy came back to our church, sometime after I had been going out on the streets. We had joined the staff of the church by that time. We had two services, and I had guests staying at my house. I had to go home between services to get the guests and bring them back to church. Randy had already started the second service, and he asked, "Where are Pete and Jenna?" I was at home getting the guests. He had a word. I don't know if he remembers this, but he had a word burning so deeply inside of him that he could not move on. He couldn't move on until I got there. Brenda called me on my cell phone and said, "You need to get back here. Randy's holding the service until you get back. He has to prophesy over you." He just wept as he shared God's heart for what we were doing. He shared some really beautiful things. Even then we didn't realize what God was doing.

Randy looked at us and said, "You can never boast in what's happening. You always need to remember that you can never boast in what's happening, because this is completely the grace of God on you. This is completely a sovereign act of God on you. There's never to be any boasting." I remember him telling the church not to be envious that he was spending so much time with us. He said, "What's happening to them is what's happening to the Body."

It wasn't just about us. It was such wisdom. Pete and I still remember that word. What we have been called to has nothing to do with what we did. It was just the goodness of God, the grace of God on us.

In 2002, we went to Mozambique with Global Awakening. At that time, only pastors could go out into the bush. I remember women couldn't go, because they didn't have accommodations for them. For that reason, women had to stay at the compound, and the men would go. I remember praying, "I just want to go, I just want to go," and the door opened and they allowed me to go out into the bush with everyone.

It was just such an amazing experience. At that point, all of the 12 pastors were with Heidi and Rolland, and they all prayed over us. All the children and Heidi and Rolland prayed over us. We knew then that there was an impartation of something.

At one Voice of the Apostles conference, we heard Bill Johnson say, "If you just see somebody and admire them for their faith, but it stays at admiration and you never duplicate what's made your heart leap, it's a sin. It's an injustice." He said that we have the responsibility to put what we see into action in our own lives. We might not be able to do what Heidi and Rolland did—go to Africa and care for thousands of orphans. But we could adopt one. We could do something.

So we began the process of adoption. We just said, "Well, we'll do what we can. From then on, we would just say, "We're going to do something." So we started the process of adopting our daughter, Priscilla. She is Asian; we adopted her before we moved overseas because of the heart for adoption imparted to us while we were in Africa.

We were never "children people," even though everyone thinks that we are so anointed with kids. I never taught a Sunday school class. I never wanted to work in the nursery, nothing like that. When we were in Africa, I would just cry out, asking God to give the children parents. Then God said, "What about you?" Everything changed. What God did was huge!

Pete and I can't walk through the airport now without getting our hands on other people's babies. It's just something that God did. I mean, we were proper; we had good jobs, and we wanted life to be easy, and God just wrecked that. After what happened in Africa, we knew that there was a calling beyond what we thought.

We went back to the Voice of the Apostles conference every year. Every year God would speak to us and tell us what was on His heart and what He wanted us to do. Every year we would go home and would apply it in whatever way that we could. What we received was too precious to hold in our hands. It would be so wasteful to keep all that God had given us to ourselves. We would just do whatever He called us to, in whatever capacity that we could.

At the Voice of the Apostles in 2003, we began to feel the call to Southeast Asia. I could talk for days about how the Lord confirmed that call. We didn't know much about anything. We didn't know the language. We didn't know one person from that culture, but the Lord put it in our hearts.

Pete was completely overwhelmed by the 10/40 window, by the thought that a large portion of the world's population that had never heard the Gospel. He just sensed this was where we had to go. Where we lived, everybody had heard the Gospel and no one was really interested. We tried to witness to people in our town, and they looked at us like we were crazy.

We just had such a desire to make sure that before people died, they knew about the love of God and what had happened to us. I remember one time we went up for an altar call when Dennis Balcomb was speaking. It was the only year that he could get into the U.S., and that was the year that the Lord was stirring us about Southeast Asia.

Dennis said that on the airplane, the Lord told him that there would be somebody at Voice of the Apostles who would be launched into Asian missions. We didn't know necessarily that it was us, but I remember that at the conference, I was so radically touched by the Lord that I even spoke the language. I was completely overcome by the Holy Spirit, and there was a woman from an Asian nation standing next to me. Afterward, the lady was talking to Pete and said, "I didn't know your wife was from Asia." He said, "She's not." The lady smiled and said, "She was speaking our language." We didn't know that because we didn't know any of that particular language.

At that conference, we received a strong prophetic word from C. Hope Flinchbaugh. She said, "Write this down. This is not a prayer. This is a prophetic word from the Lord. Document this day." She then said, "The Lord says: Today I'm giving you a voice for the children in Southeast Asia."

We knew this was a word from the Lord. Our spirits leapt inside us. We felt we needed to obey quickly and go while the door was open. We knew it would be quick. It was very important that we step out while there was an open door. The nation of our hearts was open at that time., and we didn't know how long it would remain open. Doors open and close all the time. We sensed that the Lord said to go, and if we waited because we were just waiting for things to be easy, the door might close. How would God feel about that?

We completed our adoption of Priscilla in the summer of 2005, as we were preparing to go. During this season, we continued to receive prophetic words and guidance about our call.

I remember one day sitting in the back of the church. No one knew what was going in our hearts. Pete and I still do this; we don't put a lot of things out. We don't put out a lot of information or talk about money or anything like that. We just always pray. In the beginning, we didn't tell anybody about this nation or about our wanting to adopt—no one. I remember sitting in the back of the church before the service, just thinking, not even praying, "Wouldn't it be nice if someone came and confirmed this to me." Immediately, a man from the front of the church came directly back to me and said, "I had a dream about you last night. You were standing there, and you were in an Asian dress. It had little frogs down the front of it." He said that was it. I said, "What do you think that means?" He said, "I don't know. I just thought that you would be going to Southeast Asia someday." We heard that all the time.

At one point, the Lord spoke to me about going on a fast. I had been on a 40-day fast before. It was glorious and excruciating all at the same time. I remember Him speaking to me about the seriousness of this call and Him speaking to me about a 40-day fast. I couldn't do this one alone. I really felt that Pete and I were supposed to do this one together. I didn't want to mention it to Pete because he was working so hard. I said, "If it's really you, Lord, you'll have to speak to him." The next day Pete came to me and said, "I feel like we need to go on a 40-day fast." So we began this fast.

On the 38th day of the fast, an Asian man came into Englewood. No Asian people ever came into the area where we lived in Englewood. He was giving a conference on adoption, and our adoption of Priscilla was almost complete. The Lord began speaking to us about the unwanted children through dreams and confirming words from people. They were radical words from the Lord.

Pete and I had been praying about some things that were on our hearts. We wanted to work in an orphanage. We wanted to work with children whose parents were imprisoned. This man came, and he had founded an orphanage. Although he didn't live there, he supported it, and the orphanage worked with ministries that supported children whose parents were in prison. This was a very divine connection.

It was soon after this that we sold everything that we had and gave the rest away. God said to go, and so we just sold everything. We sold our house. We sold one car and gave another car away. As soon as we put our house on the market, a lady came and said, "I'll take everything, and I want it exactly the way that it is. I want your sheets; I want your silverware. You can keep the pictures in the frames, but I would like to have everything else." So that made it really easy for us. I told her there were some things that my friends wanted. Friends and family came and took what they wanted, and the rest stayed there. I gave each of my friends some of my jewelry, so they would remember me. It was so fun.

I remember my friends coming to my closet. I loved clothes and shoes. They went through my closet. I was sitting in a chair thinking how it reminded me of being at my funeral, but it wasn't sad in any way. There was no sadness. I remember this weird feeling of people going through my belongings and taking whatever they wanted. The more things we got rid of, the freer we got.

My parents had a little cabin on a river that was like a preserve. They said that we could stay there. It had one bedroom. From the time that we sold our house in November 2004 until we left for our new overseas home in February 2005, we stayed in this little cabin. It was such an amazing blessing because there were no telephones. We were out in the middle of nowhere, and God just prepared us.

When we left the U.S., we had nothing. Literally, each one of us had two suitcases that included our clothes, and the kids brought one box of Legos. We had to bring our summer and winter clothes and shoes, and that took up the majority of each of our two suitcases. We weren't storing anything. We weren't planning on coming back. We felt this was a long-term call. We didn't think we would be there for a couple of years and come back. We felt our new nation would be home.

We were such bad missionaries. We didn't know anything- not the language, not the culture, nothing. We just headed out that February with our three children, knowing we were going to the place where God had called us.

We didn't know any of the language, not one word, and we didn't have a home. We didn't have sheets; we didn't have towels. We had nothing. A lady helped us find a little apartment that was filthy and had rats in it. We had raw sewage everywhere for many months. We didn't know how to order from the menu because it wasn't in English. Our daughter was 11 months old when we adopted her, and less than a year later she was back in her home country with her new family. The kids were young—Logan was eight, Mitchell was five and Priscilla was 18 months old.

When we got there, we simply did what Heidi had told us to do. We started going to the parks, sitting with the poor, and learning the language. Shortly after arriving, we began volunteering at a local orphanage. One day I figured out how to get into the baby house at the government-sanctioned orphanage, and so I started going there. They really did not like any foreigners going there. The first time they tolerated me, but as I started to come back repeatedly, they didn't seem to like that. They wouldn't let me hold any babies. They never held the babies. No one ever held the babies.

I started to bring the nurses fruit. I decided since they wouldn't let me serve the babies, then I'd serve the staff. I started by bringing fruit, but I also helped make bottles. There were so many babies with cleft palates. I tried to get special bottles from the States. We would go into the orphanage, and it was eerily quiet.

The babies don't cry because crying doesn't get them anything. They learn very quickly that crying doesn't make any difference, so they don't cry. They're put in a room when they first come because they are crying, and the staff doesn't want the crying babies to disturb the other babies. When they learn to stop crying, they are moved into the room with the other children.

As a speech language pathologist by trade, I had worked in the States in a hospital neo-natal unit that had small infants who had swallowing disorders. I had only one cleft palate case, because this birth defect is not as common in the States. When I would walk into the orphanage in Asia, I would hear a certain sound of breathing and gurgling. Babies there lay on a flat board, a piece of wood. I would walk in and hear this drowning sound. All the babies were drowning in their formula because the staff would cut off the tops of the nipples and stick them in these itty, bitty babies' mouths. They weren't able to move their heads when they were finished drinking. All you would hear was babies drowning because they couldn't get the bottle of milk to stop pouring in their little mouths.

I kept thinking, "If we could just sit the babies up." I was praying, "God, just let me teach them some of my speech stuff." I knew that some things were just a matter of education and communication. I knew that if you hold a baby at a certain degree, that the drinking could be better, and even if the staff didn't want to hold the babies, then maybe they could prop pillows up for them.

At the orphanage, they didn't burp the babies, so what the babies did get down, they ended up vomiting back up. As a result, the babies were severely malnourished. In fact, many were dying, and everyone seemed to consider this normal, no big deal.

In my heart, I asked God to one day give me an opportunity to teach them basic tips, like propping the babies up on pillows, giving them the right kind of bottles, and burping them. Until that opportunity came (and it did!), I determined I would just go and serve there.

One day there was this little baby girl, and she was crying. She was so itty bitty that I could fit her in my hand. I said to one of the nurses, "Can I please hold her?" She said, "Yeah, sure, go ahead," and she let me pick her up. I immediately heard the voice of Lord like I had never heard it before. I heard Him say, "Tell her that I heard her cry, and that's why I sent you."

That message has stuck with us throughout our time here, because it is as simple as that. It's not that we are some big faith people, missionaries. It was He who heard a baby cry, and He who sent somebody. All we did was say, "Yes." That was it, so beautifully simple.

That thought has kept us in check if we ever start to think that we're doing something. No, He heard them cry, and He sent us.

After we had been there for three months, we had to leave the country and go to another country to get our visa renewed, because we were only able to get a tourist visa, and those have to be renewed every three months. We were told there was a lot of theft at that time in Hong Kong, so we should not bring any money into the city and should use our ATM card once we got there. Bring a little bit of cash, but get the rest when you get there was the advice.

Everything in Hong Kong was extraordinarily expensive. Hong Kong is the fourth most expensive city in the world, which we didn't know because we didn't know much about anything. We just thought it would be like where we were serving, very cheap. So we went to renew our visas with a little bit of money and realized that the cost of the taxi from the airport to the hotel would take every penny we had. We didn't have anybody with us to help us, we didn't know the language, and we had three kids with us.

We went to get money out of the ATM, and all the ATM's were locked up because there had been credit card theft, and no one was allowed to take money out. There we were in Hong Kong without a penny. We couldn't have money wired to us. We had no money to get our visas, no money to take a taxi or a bus to get from our hotel to the visa office, no money for food, no money to pay for the hotel, and we were already checked into the hotel.

I went into the bathroom and just cried because my kids were saying, "Mommy, I'm hungry. We're hungry." I said I didn't know what to do, and I didn't want them to see me cry. So I went into the bathroom and cried and prayed.

Pete went for a walk and came across this little Christian bookstore. I think Lesley-Anne Leighton or Heidi Baker had given us a card with the names of people they knew in Hong Kong. Well, it was the same people who ran this little Christian bookstore! He went in, and they could tell there was something wrong.

They started ministering to Pete and asked what was going on. I don't know what he told them. He just started explaining the predicament we were in. They gave him money and helped with everything that we needed. The woman in the bookstore also handed him a book called The House of Loving Faithfulness.

I had been touched by orphans and their lives, but this book was something completely different. The woman at the bookstore had said to Pete, "This is from God," and she just gave him the book. The book told the story of two women who had come to Hong Kong and given their whole lives to take care of severely disabled children in Hong Kong. These children were mentally handicapped, locked in cages, and had no arms and no legs. I remember reading through it, and I could feel God inviting me.

I had no vision, and it wasn't like we had been given a vision to go open an orphanage or work with special needs kids. I knew I wanted to help, but I liked working on the streets. I liked ministering to the prostitutes. That's what I thought I was called to, but I also had this new impartation of love for orphans that came from Father's heart.

I read the book and again I could feel the Lord inviting me. He wasn't demanding. He was inviting me into it-- this new laid-down life. I knew my Father's voice by now. This was how He had talked to me and invited me into each thing.

My heart was pounding; I started crying and said, "I don't think I have that kind of love. You're talking about children that drool. They're not the lovely cute little babies, and they're incontinent. They're severely disabled, and it's not what I had pictured doing."

I was being real with God. I remember Him drawing me to that. I said, "Oh God, I know that I don't have that kind of love inside of me, but I know that You do." I said, "I'm telling You right now, I will never say 'No,' to You. If You want this, if this is the picture that You have of my life, I say, 'Yes.'" I was afraid because I knew what He would do. He never turns down a "Yes!"

That was Saturday. On Sunday, we flew back to our new foreign home and received a phone call from some Christian ladies. They had this little premature baby whom they had found on a road in the country. They had had him for three days. He had a severe, bi-lateral complete cleft lip and cleft palate. He also had something severely wrong with his brain. He had ambiguous sex- you could not tell if he was a girl or a boy- and he had a hole in his heart. He could fit in my hand.

They called us and said, "We have this baby, and we can't feed him. He's dying. He's a premature newborn, and he hasn't eaten in three days, just the little bit of drops we could fit in his mouth." They told us that they had fasted and prayed for three days, and they were flipping through their phone book and came to the name of an Asian lady who just happened to be one who helped us get our sheets and our towels when we first arrived. They asked her, "Do you know anyone who could help?" She said that the only thing she could think of was an American couple who said that they had a heart for orphans. She suggested the women call us.

It was Sunday when they called and said, "We'll bring him on Tuesday." I said, "We obviously need time to prepare, but if he's not eating, he'll be dead by Tuesday. Bring him now." We named him Caleb.

Wrapped in a towel, he was covered from his head to his toes in blisters because they had no been able to clean him after he was born. He couldn't eat anything by himself. However, just the week before, a friend of mine from the States had sent me a box. She had heard that I was going to see the babies in the government orphanage with cleft lips and palates, so the box she sent included cleft bottles and nipples, preemie diapers, a special infant power kick formula for neonates, and a diaper bag with preemie clothes in it. Everything that I needed for this little baby was in this box!

As I uncovered this little skeleton of a baby, I remember thinking, "I want to do this for the rest of my life." It just became the most glorious thought. I had never seen anything so filled with the glory of the Lord as this little baby. Unwrapping the towel from around him was like unwrapping the glory of the Lord. I couldn't believe what was happening in my heart. I couldn't believe what God was doing in my heart, because it wasn't me. All I had to do was say "Yes," and "I trust you." He not only sent us our first disabled, orphaned baby immediately, but He gave us everything that we needed to follow His voice.

Shortly after we returned from Hong Kong, we asked if we could have the child I had first held at the orphanage. She was two months old and had only been held by me. The government said, "No." We said, "Okay, thank you for considering that." We didn't argue, we didn't make a fuss, we just asked for her.

Now, we had already taken in Caleb, but the memory of that baby girl I was allowed to hold stayed with me. That's why we asked to take her home. The orphanage staff did not understand why we wanted two babies, because most families in their nation will only foster one child. They denied our request for a second little foster baby, this little girl.

When we got home after they told us no, Pete and I got down on our faces, crying out to God. The Lord gave me the Scripture in Proverbs 21:1 that says, "The king's heart is a stream of water in the hand of the Lord; he turns it wherever he will."[28] I said, "God, You said that the government is like water in Your hands. So if this is You, and You want this baby in our hands, turn it in our favor." That became our life's prayer: Turn the favor of Your hand towards us, because kings and governments are only water. We prayed and just poured out our heart to the Lord.

Two weeks later, the orphanage called us and asked, "Do you still want that baby? You can have her." From then on, for every child we were allowed to foster, we would have the same conversation with the Lord. The government would say, "Jenna, this is impossible," and "Pete, this is impossible. This has never been done before, and this is impossible. There's no way that you can do this." We would go home and pray. The timeframe always seemed to be one-and-a-half to two weeks. The response would always change to "You can have" whatever it was we asked for.

Soon after those first few babies came home, we began to focus on opening a home for children who seemed to have no hope for living or no family. God opened many doors for us to minister. Although it is very uncommon in our nation for non-nationals to own a house, it is even more uncommon for them to own a plot of land, yet God has given us one. Today our Special Blessings Children's Home not only has a main housing area for all the children, it also has several other buildings that serve as prayer rooms, guest housing, and healing rooms (based on the John G. Lake Healing Rooms model).

[28] RSV

I want to share with you some of the stories of the children who have especially touched our lives. God has done many miracles to bring them to us and to sustain them.

Aaron is a baby who was stolen from his parents when he was a day or two old. Sometimes a boy is taken from his family and put up for sale. Often the wealthy want to buy a boy, because eventually he will be the provider for the family. This boy was taken from the countryside, and we don't even know which province he came from. He ended up in a big city near where we are, and when I went to the orphanage one day I saw him, so stiff that even when he was resting, his back couldn't rest on the bed. He had a severe form of cerebral palsy because when he was smuggled across a border, he was put into a small box so no one would find him. He didn't have enough air for days, which caused severe brain damage. He is a gorgeous baby. Can you imagine what it must have been like for him? He was probably screaming in this little box.

Of course, nobody wanted him. When children are taken like that, they have no hope of anything. There's no hope of being adopted because they are considered the property of the police, just in case they ever find the children's real parents. They also cannot go into foster homes. Their destiny is to spend their lives in an orphanage, with a staff who are often poorly trained and where living conditions are unbearable.

After I saw the "taken" boy for the first time, I said, "I want him." They said, "You're crazy. Not even native families can come in and take this baby. It's impossible. Jenna, don't even ask about this one." At that time, with all the other children, we had 12 special needs kids with severe problems. But each one of them was handpicked. God would just highlight and rescue them.

It was amazing. Pete and I were exhausted and were up all day and all night. We were spent, just spent- just like Randy's message said, "Spend and Be Spent." In the midst of all this, I still saw this baby, and they would say, "No." Every time before this when they said, "No," I would just say "Okay, thank you," and go home and pray, and the Lord would open the door.

This time I intended to do the same thing, but God said, "No, I want you to be as the persistent widow. I want you to ask and keep asking." So I did. Every time I heard from the orphanage or the government, I would ask about this baby. They would say, "No, you can't have this baby. Don't ask about it again." The next time I would say, "Remember that baby?" They were getting so frustrated with me; I was getting a little nervous. I was saying, "God, is this You or is this me?" Just because we're out in the mission field, doesn't mean that we can't still step out in our flesh and make mistakes. So, at this point, I was questioning everything.

I stayed persistent for three months. We were about to get another group of three babies that the orphanage had said "Yes" to. But by faith I was still thinking about that little one. God never forgets, not one. This baby couldn't give us anything. He couldn't even look at us or give us smiles. He was in such terrible shape, but God saw him, and He would not let us relent.

Our whole staff fasted and prayed. Everything we do involves our whole staff—never just Pete and me. We knew we were getting three babies, but I bought cribs for four. I just knew he was going to come home with us. When I went to the government office to sign the foster care papers, the contract was for the three babies. I asked again. I had a good relationship with one of the leaders there, so I asked her. I said, "I am signing these contracts for these three, but what about this little guy?" And she said, "Jenna, I told you 'No,' and do not ask me again." Her voice told me that she was serious. I had crossed the line, and I was afraid of breaking the relationship because the nationals have such a relational culture. You have to have relationship, otherwise, you won't be able to get anything. The laws don't matter; you have to have the relationships.

So we got back in the van that day, taking three home, not four. I was just crying out to the Lord, "Did I make a mistake? Please check my heart." And I firmly heard Him say, "No, I told you to be the persistent widow, so just pray." I prayed the whole way home. The next day the phone rang, and they said, "You can have the baby." I went and picked him up that very day. That's happened so many times.

The Lord asked me, "Who will be the voice? Who will stand in and not accept a 'No'?" The local government seems so fierce, really intimidating, but God says, "Who will believe in My government? If I say 'No,' then fine. But I didn't say 'No.' I said 'Yes.'" Repeatedly, He reminded me that He will do anything. He will do anything if only someone will stand in the gap—not just for a little while, but for as long as it takes to contend and persist.

What's this little dying baby ever going to give us until the Lord heals him? Nothing. It's not like he was a cute little lovely baby. He couldn't even have a bowel movement by himself. We had to help him do everything. God obviously wanted him in our care. His name is Aaron, and he is beautifully alive today.

Actually, they gave Aaron to us for a trial period. The government officials said they would visit Special Blessings Home after a month to see if he'd made any improvement. If not, they would take him back. So when we got home, we prayed and prayed and prayed and pretty soon his little body began to loosen up. After a month, a number of men came to check out Special Blessings Home and to see Aaron. He was sitting in a little bouncy seat with his body curved, and the doctors just stood there and stared at him and said, "Truly, this is a miracle. This baby could not move a muscle." He was completely relaxed, with his back bending normally in his seat. They had had him for months, and they said to us, "You can have him for as long as you want him." We have had him for three years now.

Another of our children, **Sonny**, helped open doors with the orphanages, changing our relationships with them. We visited an orphanage we'd never been to, so we could meet the leaders and develop a relationship with them. We weren't planning to take any children because we were just beginning to get to know the orphanage staff.

We were there for four hours, and they took us on a tour of the facility. It was just horrible, but you cannot show any emotion. People have asked me, "How do you do that? I would never be able to do that." I asked the Lord that one time, and He said, "If you don't go, then who's going to go?" He showed me, "If you go, I'll give you the grace to go. Don't tell Me that you can't go because I see them every single day. Would you please join with Me to get them out?" I realized that God has to see these kids and has to watch as nobody goes to help them.

While at the orphanage, we saw a little boy sitting in a corner. He was 11 years old, completely blind, and had severe autism. He was sitting in a corner and was the toy for all the other children. They came and whacked him on the head and smacked him. Because he was blind, he couldn't see anything coming. He kept his hands over his head, and they would come and stomp on his feet. Because he couldn't see it coming, he was constantly scared, waiting for the next blow. That ripped my heart out. I watched him sitting on this little stool for four hours while he was being abused.

I looked at Pete, and something rose up inside of me. I knew it was the Lord, and it was the word "Enough." It was enough. It was too much. We had no experience with any of the disabilities that the children we cared for had except the cleft lips. I didn't know anything about taking care of a blind child with autism or anything like that. But I heard the Scripture in my mind, "Suppose a brother or sister is without clothes and daily food. If one of you says to him, 'Go, I wish you well; keep warm and well fed,' but does nothing about his physical needs, what good is it?"[29] As soon as my eyes locked on this boy, God highlighted him. He became my responsibility.

Pete and I looked at each other, and I said, "I want to take him. How about you?" "Yeah, I want to take him too," he said. So we asked, and they let us take him, no contract or paperwork. We just walked out with this child. We had a driver because we didn't know where we were going. The orphanage was four hours from our house, and we didn't know the roads there.

Pete and I were sitting in the back seat of the car with this young boy, and we named him Sonny. We pray about every name we give a child while they are in our care. Sonny was sitting on Pete's lap, and he was the sweetest little thing, all snuggled up. Pete and I were like proud parents bringing our first baby home from the hospital. There was just glory in the car. I can't even describe what it was like. We were laughing and touching him and singing, just doing all this stuff that Moms and Dads do.

As soon as he stepped one foot on our property, we knew there was an open heaven over us, just a glorious atmosphere. At the same time, Sonny went ballistic. He became unglued. He was the most demonized child I have ever seen in my entire life. I mean he was violent, incredibly violent.

Anytime we would pray for him, he would scream and not in a normal voice. It was demonic. He would find any hard surface,

---

[29] James 2:15-16, NIV

which was easy to do since we don't have carpet or anything soft, and bang his head and his whole body—on floors, toilets, or bathtubs. He would just scream and scratch himself. He was completely black and blue and raw. He would self-mutilate all the time.

He threw toys, hit babies, and hurt people. He would go to the bathroom all over everything and smear it everywhere. He would refuse to eat and drink, and we thought he was going to die. He would clench his mouth shut and refuse to eat anything. The enemy had a powerful assignment to kill this child, and it was torture to watch. He wouldn't sleep. As soon as the sun went down, he would really come unglued and screech and scream. He would contort in a clearly demonic way.

We tried everything we could to get him to sleep. But he never slept for more than two or three hours every night. We tried a tent, a bed, and a pack 'n play. We tried everything. He would get out of bed and tear everything up in a matter of seconds. We were afraid that he was going to fall down the stairs and hurt himself.

Finally Pete and I put him in between us, and we had to sleep with our arms locked up and Sonny in between. He would even slip out of that, like a little snake, he was so demonized. He would kind of slither and get out as quickly as he could, and wreck the place. Because of his blindness, he just knocked everything over; one time he even gave me a black eye!

Our staff was afraid of him. People came to me and said, "Jenna, you are in over your head. You don't know anything about taking care of a child with a problem this severe." I would just say, "You're right, I don't." I never claimed to know what I was doing, but I said, "What is the alternative?" Leave him here or send him back? What would you do? What about the Good Samaritan? What do you do about that? I couldn't just say, "Peace be with you," and walk away.

I could feel God's heart for this child. We fasted and prayed for three months, and he was just horrific. He was losing weight. We could get a little bit of food in him, but he was so skinny because he refused to eat anything and was not sleeping. Pete and I were not sleeping either, and we were exhausted.

One night it was so bad that I decided to bring him downstairs to an empty room where there were mats on the floor. I sat crossed legged, so I could put him in my lap, and I restrained him. I said, "God, I don't know what to do." I started questioning myself: "Am I in over my head?" I didn't think I was, but I was just trying to search my heart.

All I heard was the song, "How Great Is Our God. Sing with me." So I began to sing this song over him, and I was just crying and singing. As I watched, his whole body suddenly went limp. For the first time in three months, he was relaxed. All of a sudden, I saw his little hand come up, and he touched his cheek. I looked over at his face, and he had a tear coming down.

Pretty soon he didn't know what was happening to him. An emotion like that had never come out. He was completely dumbfounded by this, and he began weeping. I just sang louder, "How Great Is Our God" over and over. I don't even know how long I just rocked and sang over him until he was just completely calm.

After that, bam, everything began breaking open. The first thing we noticed was that the next day, when I offered him a piece of banana to try, he opened up his mouth. Only a little, but it was huge to us. A couple days went by, and he began drinking. A few days after that, he started to go to the bathroom appropriately; he would go on the potty.

At that time, he was on a very strong sleeping medication so powerful it could have knocked an elephant out, but Sonny was only sleeping two to three hours before this happened. Pete saw that Sonny was doing so well and he said, "I think we should try to take him off his meds," because he had started sleeping through the night. "I'm going to sleep downstairs in the tent with him (we have so many mosquitoes that you have to sleep in a mosquito tent) and let you get some sleep. We won't give him the medication, and we'll see what happens."

He slept all through the night. His behavior was calm and really peaceful. About a week later he stood up. No one will ever forget it. He stood up in the living room, and he started dancing and going in circles, saying, "Happy, happy, happy!" in English. "Jesus makes me happy! Happy, happy, happy!"

He said that for months. He would get up and go in circles and say over and over with a huge smile on his face, "Happy, happy, happy! Jesus makes me happy!" He never had another fit, ever. He is everyone's favorite child. He still has autistic characteristics, and he is still blind, but he is not tormented anymore. We pray daily for his eyes. I really want him to see. But the tormenting behaviors have stopped, and that may be one of our biggest miracles ever.

Children come and go at Special Blessings. We meet them with love and prayer and expect that they will have a testimony of the miraculous in their lives.

One little guy was born with cerebral palsy, a cleft lip, and a cleft palate. He was being placed for adoption, but they didn't tell his prospective mother that anything was wrong with his brain or development. They just told her about the cleft lip and cleft palate. When she came to pick him up, he was flat and rigid. She kept him three days in her hotel room, and during that time he couldn't pick up his head, even though he was a year and a half. He couldn't do anything.

This mother had adopted before, so she knew that kids who have spent time in an orphanage often have developmental delays and need some time to catch up, but this was beyond what she had experienced. He was completely unresponsive. He couldn't eat; he couldn't do anything. On the third day, she took him to a pediatric neurologist in our city, who diagnosed him with severe mental retardation and cerebral palsy. He would never walk, he would never talk, and he wouldn't be able to feed himself.

She was devastated as she had come all the way around the world to adopt this baby. She was a single mom, and she didn't believe that she had what it took to adopt a child who had a severe disability. The government decided to search for another baby boy for her, and that search brought her to our home. At the time, we had two boys who were very healthy, and she wound up adopting Samson.

Pete and I asked about the other baby boy. "What about him?" We were told, "Oh, he'll go back to the orphanage on the mentally handicapped ward, and he will spend his life there" (which is horrific, to say the least). Pete and I said, "Can we have him?" At that time, we weren't allowed to foster children anywhere else except in our city. It was illegal to take in foster children outside your area. This was a new orphanage, one of the poorest orphanages I've ever seen, and it was far away. We had to petition for this baby.

We ended up getting him. I have pictures of him. He had sores all over his private parts and face, and he had a totally flat appearance—no emotion or response on his face at all. Within four days, we saw a smile and after that, we just prayed, prayed, prayed, and prayed over this child. He began reaching developmental milestones, and pretty soon he caught up with all the other children. His cleft lip and palate were repaired surgically. He was walking, talking, running, eating, and playing. In fact, we found him to be one of the brightest children in our preschool class. Just recently, a family adopted him!

If God hadn't sent us here, he would still be in one of the most horrific places for children in this country. But God had a plan, and now this little boy has a beautiful family that loves the Lord, and he is completely restored and healed. It is such a great testimony!

We've seen God respond with other miracles as well—even a doctor fresh out of medical school healed of Hepatitis B. A girl born with albinism—no color in her eyes or body—was healed of blindness.

There are many stories we could tell—of baby formula arriving in the middle of the night to feed hungry babies, of a car full of birthday gifts appearing at just the right moment to fill children with hope and joy.

We've also seen God work in relationship with the government and with the foreign nationals who work alongside us. With the blessing of the government, we've had opportunities to share our education and experience to bring better living conditions at the state-run orphanages, including brighter paint colors and pillows for all the babies.

That does not mean that everything is perfect or easy. We have had five babies die. The most recent occurred just last Friday while I was in the U.S. for a conference. Right before Noah died, I had a vision in which I saw him dying and many of us at Special Blessings praying for him to be raised from the dead. In the vision, he was raised, and he was completely healed. A few hours later, I got the phone call that Noah had been rushed to the hospital and had died. Our staff did pray for him, but he was not raised.

I asked the Lord why He gave me that vision when Noah was not raised. God said, "Yes, five have died- but thirty-five have lived!" I asked, "Why the vision?" He said, "I wanted to give you a foundation of *My* will. I wanted it to be set, what my will is. My will is to raise the dead. I don't want you to ever doubt it or to stop asking for it." It's about hope, even in death.

Of course, that isn't the end of the story. How many people do you know who have held any dead babies in their arms and really had to believe? There's a reason for such a promise. The vision is to tell us to continue, to go to the dying ones who have no hope, wrecked hearts, wrecked brains. The vision made it even clearer to me about our call to contend for life. Through the heartache and the anguish of losing Noah and the other four, I still can hear the Lord proposing His reality to me. He is still speaking to me that His will is always to raise the dead and bring 100 percent healing. No matter how desolate a situation is, His will is firm. He came to bring life. I have the opportunity to contend until it comes to pass. And I said, "God, keep them coming."

Endnote

Miracles and stories of God's grace abound among those who have been touched through impartation. So many have gone from just one touch to touching other lives with the Gospel, bringing healing to the hurting, reaching out to the lost, ministering to the forgotten, and saving the children no one else wants.

God gives us gifts so that we can give to others. Whatever we have received through His hand, we can give others. And that's what it's all about. Jesus told us, "As you go, preach this message: 'The kingdom of heaven is near.' Heal the sick, raise the dead, cleanse those who have leprosy, drive out demons. Freely you have received, freely give."[30]

These are the stories of just a few who've received and gone on to give. They are like the wise servant who took the five talents, gained five more, and earned the approval of his master. His reward was to share in his master's happiness and to receive greater responsibility.[31]

I know that there are many, many more like those profiled in *Changed in a Moment*. Testimonies continue to multiply and build as the Kingdom message is preached, and stories are shared. Much like the book of Acts, this book does not have an ending, because we look with great anticipation to all that God will do as He reveals more and more of His powerful goodness. For we know that, "Of the increase of his government and peace there will be no end."[32]

[30] Matthew 10:7-8, NIV
[31] Matthew 25:14-28, NIV
[32] Isaiah 9:7a, NIV

Other books by Randy Clark

Entertaining Angels

There Is More

Power, Holiness and Evangelism

Lighting Fires

God Can Use Little Ole Me

Other Booklets by Randy Clark

Evangelism Unleashed

Healing Ministry and Your Church

Learning to Minister Under the Anointing

Training Manuals Available

Ministry Team Training Manual

Schools of Healing and Impartation Workbooks

Core Message Series

Words of Knowledge

Biblical Basis of Healing

Baptism in the Holy Spirit

Open Heaven

Pressing In

The Thrill of Victory / The Agony of Defeat

In "There Is More," Randy lays a solid biblical foundation for a theology of impartation as well as taking a historical look at impartation and visitation of the Lord in the Church. This is combined with many personal testimonies of people who have received an impartation throughout the world and what the lasting fruit has been in their lives. You are taken on journey throughout the world to see for yourself the lasting fruit that is taking place in the harvest field - particularly in Mozambique. This release of power is not only about phenomena of the Holy Spirit, it is about its ultimate effect on evangelism and missions. Your heart will be stirred for more as you read this book.

"This is the book that Randy Clark was born to write."

- Bill Johnson

Global School of Supernatural Ministry

Vision
To release followers of Christ into their specific destiny and calling, in order to live out the Great Commission.

Structure
Global School of Supernatural Ministry is a one or two year ministry school with an emphasis on impartation and equipping students for a life of walking in the supernatural. Classes start each September and end the following May. Courses are offered on-site at the Apostolic Resource Center in Mechanicsburg, PA. Upon completion of each program year a Certificate of Completion is awarded. Students seeking additional educational training may do so while attending GSSM through the Wagner Leadership Institute.

Community
The GSSM student body is diverse in age, culture, ministry experience, and educational accomplishments. From high school graduates to professionals to retirees - the students come together seeking more of God. Supernatural power, passion and honor are key values of GSSM and are reflected in our worship, outreach and personal relationships.

For more information - or to enroll in classes - contact us at 1-866-AWAKENING or apply online at http://gssm.globalawakening.com

globalawakening

For a schedule of upcoming events and conferences, or to purchase other products from Global Awakening, please visit our website at:

http://www.globalawakening.com